Corporate Game Theory

Strategizing, Thinking & Playing the Corporate Game

John Mark Gray

CONTENTS

"To predict the behavior of ordinary people in advance, you only have to assume that they will always try to escape a disagreeable situation with the smallest possible expenditure of intelligence." — Friedrich Nietzsche

1 INTRODUCTION

The world of Corporate America has changed a lot from the good old days where employees stayed at the same company for 30 years until they retired with a nice pension. Employees are no longer thought of as investments with human resources departments and upper management strategically planning their development and career path in the company.

These good old days of shared loyalty between corporations and employees are long gone. Occasionally you can find a couple of employees in a large corporation who have logged 25 years with the same company, and they are given the proverbial gold watch for their long dedication and service to the firm. But these are outliers in the modern scheme of things in today's workforce.

You want to work for a large corporation because this is where all the perks, annual bonuses, best training, and highest salaries reside in the workplace. In short, go where the money is if you want the best things in life. And it isn't working for small-scale companies with little economy of scale to increase margins and monopolize a given sector in society.

You wonder why companies keep incessantly gobbling up smaller companies and merging with their peers? This is to increase economies of scale, gain more pricing power, eliminate direct competitors, gain market share, throw their weight around and make higher margins.

Since the government in the United States has basically looked the other way in terms of these mergers being great for companies and bad for consumers, only standing in the way of the highest profile acquisitions where elected officials will take a lot of heat for looking the other way, companies have continued to scale up in size and become large behemoths that dominate their industries like large planets in a solar system with enormous gravitational pull swallowing up small competitors like space rocks.

As a result, the smaller companies may have a better overall working environment, but their much smaller margins means everything is on a budget including employee perks and benefits.

So you want to work for the large Fortune 500 companies, and the bigger the better, but you need to learn how to play the game of corporate politics, and it is quite a minefield, let me tell you.

This corporate minefield will eat you up and spit you out faster than a bunch of hyenas on the plains of Africa. You may think that corporations actually care about you with all the core values propaganda promulgated on posters, desktop paperweights and company t-shirts, but it is all marketing balderdash.

You have as much value and usefulness in the organization as your boss needs you to get things done in a timely manner and can stand looking at you each day when they come to work. Moreover, even if you are the lucky few who have a great boss to work for, their boss may be squeezing them, and not be long for the corporation anyway. And all this is subject to a couple of bad earnings reports and upper management asks human resources to find savings by sending out notices to managers regarding who they can afford to lose and still keep the basic lights on in their business unit or department.

This goes for everyone in the corporation from secretaries, mid-level managers and lawyers all the way up to the executive management team, and even the CEO of the company. The only difference is that the executive management team will have better departing packages, especially at the CEO level. But giant corporations have a soul and heartbeat of their own.

The corporation runs the show and not the CEO, even though they often become disillusioned thinking they are on top of the food chain. Corporations routinely get rid of CEOs, even ones who worked their way up from lower levels and have dedicated their entire lives to the company. This can all happen faster than the drop of a hat.

It all comes down to a CYA (Cover Your Ass) mentality that permeates every aspect of Corporate America. Employees build alliances and seek out allies like a game of Survivor on an island somewhere in the tropics. They try to insulate themselves from the inevitable carnage that plays out through corporate politics with varying degrees of success, but the corporate politics environment affects everyone in the company. In short, everyone is throwing each other under the buss when it suits their interests and needs in the game of corporate survival.

Thus, as you enter the large Fortune 500 behemoths you have to learn how to play the multifaceted game of corporate politics. The better you are at navigating this corporate jungle, the more spoils and improved quality of life that can be attained throughout the long journey of your career path.

You may ask yourself, if it really is this toxic an environment, then why do I want to work in such an environment. Unless you are going to start your own company, and remember, the big behemoths today make it much harder for smaller companies to survive in our current economic environment, these corporations are where the good high-paying jobs are in our economy.

However, politics are everywhere as you cannot hide from the harsh realities of the real world in some cave in

New Mexico. So you are going to face workplace politics and be regularly tasked with socially handling different personalities in every workplace environment. It's just a unique animal regarding workplace politics in large corporations.

These are some of the most educated and smartest people on the planet, so they are going to set sophisticated traps to sabotage your career, make you look bad on a given project, and make you the fall guy for their incompetence. Therefore, it is a different type of subtle, sophisticated gamesmanship that takes place at corporations versus other workplaces.

But every social environment from high school to your local neighborhood as a kid, to that of prisons, children's daycare, team sports and academia all have their own complex dynamics full of internal politics and rules that are required for playing the games unique to each environmental paradigm.

In short, there is no escaping the game of social politics, so you might as well embrace it, and learn to play the game better than your competitors. And trust me, they may act as your friends at work, you probably think you have true friends at work, but this is largely a delusion on your part, none of these coworkers are truly your friends.

As in everything, there are some occasional exceptions to the rule, but be wary of even these friendships, because when times get tough you might find out that you were a mere convenience to have usefulness during the good times. I realize this is quite a cynical view of humanity, and people in general, but Corporate America seems to bring out some of the worst qualities in humanity.

Corporations in America aren't that much different than prisons, nobody is physically shanking you for disrespecting them in the yard, but make no mistake, there is plenty of backstabbing going on in corporations.

All the emotions and practices of jealousy, intimidation,

controlling, putting people in their place, gossiping, sabotaging, devaluing and domination all play out in the everyday world of Corporate America. It is just done in a more nuanced, subtle manner like Chinese water torture where you lose sleep at night rehashing your workplace activities and environment where you are losing the battle of corporate politics in a definitively devastating manner.

Well you are going to have to recognize that this is all a game in the first place, then you need to learn and recognize the rules of the corporate game, and finally figure out how you can play the game better for the advancement of your personal career.

There are definite better ways of playing the game, worse ways of playing the game, better strategies, worse strategies, and a whole lot of game theory calculations that play out every day in Corporate America these days.

In this book I am not going to sugarcoat things, tell you things that I think you will like hearing, or spinning things and realities the way upper management routinely does in an almost salesman like fashion, my aim is not to tell you how things should be, but how things actually are in Corporate America.

You will find that there is a large gap between the balderdash that is commonly spewed out by human resources, company mantras, value statements, company town hall meetings and the real world of how things actually get done and are rewarded or punished in Corporate America.

Everything you hear from company representatives espousing corporate values is basically marketing propaganda with the purpose of painting a corporate picture from an ideal world in some parallel universe but has little to do with how things actually work in the real world of Corporate America.

In fact, almost all the Fortune 500 companies have the same cliché five or six core values that are as useful as

Duck and Cover slogans during the Cold War era.[1] They sound great, and are wonderful in principle, and good to keep as many people in line as possible, but are routinely violated with impunity by those who have power within the corporation.

In short, if you are looking or expecting those above you in power relationships in Corporate America, including human resources to abide by or uphold the corporation's core values in your dealings with these individuals or entities you are in for a rude awakening. These core values are basically for show only although no one within the corporation will ever say this or tell you this fact publicly.

It is all part of the game, there are just certain unsaid truths that you need to recognize, that no one will ever come out directly and tell you the truth. By virtue of the fact that propagating and promoting the corporate balderdash has value and utility for the corporation itself. The Corporation has a life of its own, it's bigger than the employees, CEOs, board members and even the shareholders.

Rules are followed, rules are arbitrarily broken, people come and go, corporations become bankrupt, they get acquired in a merger, they have scandals, but as long as there is a corporate entity which is large in nature, the corporation itself holds all the power. The corporation's survival is all that matters, and everyone else is easily replaceable, including board members and CEOs, and everyone is subservient to the needs and interests of the Corporation.

Once the bureaucratic structure is put in place, the rules of the game dictate, that everything is sacrificed for the sake of the bureaucracy. This is what I mean by the thought that corporations seem to be living organisms which

---

[1] https://www.theleadermaker.com/core-values-enron/; https://en.wikipedia.org/wiki/Duck_and_Cover_(film)

transcend the individuals working for the needs of the corporation. Everyone in the end is sacrificed for the good of the Corporation.

Now you start to understand some of the background regarding why working for Corporate America is really just playing one giant game with your livelihood and career at stake each and every day. This is high stakes game theory at play here in adeptly navigating the world of corporate politics in order to survive the constant battling that goes on in Corporate America.

2 HUMAN RESOURCES

In this chapter we will discuss Human Resources Departments which have basically become glorified secretarial services for managers. In essence, the support group for the management function. To put it another way, the only function of HR in Corporate America is to clean up after and protect the management team. The human resources department is not the "advocate of employees" like the corporate propaganda wants you to believe.

As I write this chapter of the book, Google was in the news, and I thought the news summed up the reality regarding human resources departments in corporations these days. So the Equal Employment Opportunity Commission is investigating Google for allegedly discriminating against an employee because she was pregnant.

Here are some of the details regarding the complaint:

> Chelsey Glasson, a former user experience researcher who worked at Alphabet's Google for five years, wrote an internal memo that went viral last summer called "I'm Not Returning to Google After Maternity Leave, and Here is Why." In it, she alleged her supervisor made discriminatory remarks about pregnant women. She also claimed that the company retaliated against her with poor

performance ratings and unfairly denied her a
leadership position.[2]

The actual case details weren't what piqued my interest
about the case, it is the following:

> Glasson told CNBC in December that Google's
> human resources department did not investigate her
> complaint until after she hired an attorney, adding
> that she was never interviewed by HR before
> Google said it did not find her claims credible. At
> the time, Google didn't respond to requests for
> comment.[3]

This is so typical of human resources departments in
Corporate America, as they never have the back of
employees. But more striking is the fact that they are not
even trying terribly hard to cover their ass in this case.
They probably have been getting away with treating
employees like second class citizens compared to
management that they didn't even thoroughly investigate
the claim, i.e., the employee's version of events in detail
isn't that important to our findings in the case.

Sort of like putting an employee on PIP without giving
them a real chance to defend themselves as to whether this
is in fact a legitimate case of an employee severely
underperforming, or just a case of a vindictive and
overzealous manager using PIP to capriciously punish an
employee because they don't like them, or need to throw
somebody from the department under the bus to cover for
the manager's terrible performance on the job.

---

[2] https://www.cnbc.com/2020/02/19/google-pregnancy-
discrimination-case-under-investigation-by-eeoc.html
[3] https://www.cnbc.com/2020/02/19/google-pregnancy-
discrimination-case-under-investigation-by-eeoc.html

Despite all the corporate rhetoric, employees are second class citizens, and have extraordinarily little actual rights on the job. And it literally takes getting lawyers involved before these corporations start actually doing their jobs and conducting real, legitimate investigations into employee claims regarding unfair treatment.

However, there is more regarding Google's history from the same report in the following which also caught my attention:

> The latest investigation comes as Alphabet-owned Google faces multiple investigations from federal agencies as complaints by former Google employees mount. CNBC first reported that The U.S. National Labor Relations Board began an investigation into Google after the firing of four employees. That came just months after the company reached a labor settlement with the agency. Last summer, Google settled a class action age discrimination lawsuit, agreeing to pay $11 million.[4]

Remember these discrimination claims are against Google, which is a corporation based in California, is in the technology space, and definitely skews liberal, millennial facing, and literally caters to employees more than most Fortune 500 companies. California is not a right to work state like Texas, and in general employees just have more rights and options available to them than most employees at other companies in different regions of the country. And this same kind of human resources behavior is taking place there, where for all intents and purposes, it is still the "Us and Them" mentality that exists between management and

---

[4] https://www.cnbc.com/2020/02/19/google-pregnancy-discrimination-case-under-investigation-by-eeoc.html

everybody else who we will classify as employees.

Managers feel this power that Human Resources always have their back, and frankly they abuse this power. What did Albert Einstein say about power, "The attempt to combine wisdom and power has only rarely been successful and then only for a short while."[5] Human Resources should actually be there to provide a "checks and balances" against the power of managers who are in a position to regularly abuse their authority, and routinely treat employees unfairly because they know they can get away with it due to the fact that Human Resources just rubber stamps all their actions, behaviors, and decisions.

I see this mentality all the time in corporations, and I just shake my head. Where do they get these people, we studied this in graduate management classes, and it is studied in every MBA program, regarding process, procedure, and proper management theory. The problem is that there are a whole lot of managers who have never been through a rigorous MBA program with management classes, and corporations don't send employees through rigorous management trainee programs like they used to do in the 1950s through the 1980s epoch.

This glorious era of good management trainee programs at corporations ended with recessions in the 1980s, and in came the era of cost cutting, and all the companies just followed the latest trend of getting rid of these important programs. Thus, there are a lot of managers who are untrained, have no understanding of management theory, and just think that if they intimidate their employees enough by being cold and mean-spirited that they will be good workers.

The problem is that human resources and management have been pretty successful with this strategy over the years of just denying employees real due diligence in thoroughly

---

[5] https://www.brainyquote.com/quotes/albert_einstein_148800

investigating cases and claims by employees. Moreover, not enough employees go through the trouble of hiring a lawyer, most of these companies have a team of high-priced lawyers, and many outside law firms have conflicts of interests, so the end result is that employees just don't follow through with very many legal cases against corporations.

It is extremely hard to win these cases, and it is hard to get lawyers even willing to take your case as an employee because this isn't like a product liability case where the payoff can be enormous for these lawyers. In short, the risk reward isn't really there for many lawyers to take these types of employment discrimination and abuse of power cases.

The end result is that human resources just continues the same old strategy of having the managers backs in any dispute with employees, and only gets pushback in a few cases every now and then, they obviously are happy with this strategy. I imagine Google isn't happy with this latest publicity, but that's what they really care about, corporations don't really care about their employees despite the corporate rhetoric when push comes to shove.

Thus cue the corporate balderdash statement which is so cliché and commonplace at every corporation these days:

> Reporting misconduct takes courage and we want to provide care and support to people who raise concerns. All instances of inappropriate conduct reported to us are investigated rigorously, and over the past year we have simplified how employees can raise concerns and provided more transparency into the investigations process at Google.[6]

---

[6] Google spokesperson wrote in an email.
https://www.cnbc.com/2020/02/19/google-pregnancy-discrimination-case-under-investigation-by-eeoc.html

I am not trying to single out Google here, they are just symptomatic of the bigger problem that exists at all Fortune 500 companies these days, and most companies in America. The quality of leadership, the quality of relationships, the quality of managers, and the overall internal structure of corporations these days is really poor. Human Resources has become the posterchild for this organizational neglect and dysfunction at the workplace.

Human Resources Departments have become shadows of their former selves in the corporation, the least talented people work in these departments, no wonder, given their lack of "value-added" responsibilities in the corporate hierarchy these days. They basically do the bidding of management, cover the ass of the corporation as a whole, make sure they follow the regulatory formalities in regard to employee rights, cater to the manager's every need, and have morphed into glorified electronic paper pushers.

What they should be doing from a "value-add" standpoint is diligently analyzing all the employees and their requisite strengths and weaknesses, build development programs along with managers to strengthen the skillsets of employees, and provide analysis of how to properly allocate and promote talent to cover the corporation's future needs in house.

Instead, employees move around from company to company like wandering nomads because corporations do such a poor job of developing them in-house and creating a legitimate path for career development and advancement, that they try to interview for their next job and promotion at another company. This is terrible because all the resources, internal training and legacy knowledge walks out the door to the other company.

The American Corporation provides some training classes, but basically leaves it up to the manager to develop the employees and provide a career development plan. The manager usually holds this as a power carrot over the heads of employees, and typically does an extremely poor job of properly developing their employees for future opportunities with the company.

Managers will typically say when employees want to take training, "Don't you have enough to do Janis?" The incentive is in reality an inherent conflict of interest for the manager to actually develop their employees and serves as a disincentive under the current corporate structure. Make no mistake, this isn't about what the best process is to properly develop employees from a career development standpoint, it is all about having a low, bare bones cost-structure which saves the company money. It is all about the short-term money which invariably leads to short sighted thinking in corporations these days.

So when they need their talent, the corporation just puts up a job description on their website and external job boards, and they get some employee from another company who they don't even know, and probably isn't developed properly for the role. The irony is that this external candidate's Human Resources Department is in the same boat, and this employee is looking to jump ship for the same reason that the original company couldn't find any internal candidates.

The obvious ubiquitous elephant in the room is a dearth of adequate employee development programs and long-range talent planning at American Corporations. The self-fulfilling incompetency feedback loop is rather hilarious, if it wasn't so debilitating, inefficient and an accurate measure of the incompetent state of corporations these days.

Literally, corporations these days are the most chaotic, inefficient, careless, and incompetent organizational structures they have ever been in the history of modern American Business.

I realize it might seem like I am being overly harsh on

managers, but one should expect more from managers, they are paid very well versus rank and file employees, and frankly these are much easier jobs with a lot more power, a lot less pressurized work, and there is a reason workers want to get these jobs.

Furthermore, we should expect more from managers than rank and file employees, and I am much harder on managers than employees. And trust me, there are just so many bad and completely incompetent managers in Corporate America today, that it is mindboggling how these individuals get these managerial jobs to begin with.

It used to be that individuals who exhibited the right types of people and managerial skills were steered into these roles, but today you have the antithesis of personalities fit for managing people and processes filling many of these positions, and it is no wonder that these become complete train wrecks with all the direct reports hating their manager's guts.

Corporations and Human Resources should do a much better job of holding managers accountable for "problem employees" than just taking the easy way out and blaming everything on the lowly rank and file personnel. So you are telling me that all the direct reports who hate their manager's guts are the problem, who hired these people in the first place? This says a lot about the manager in my opinion. Indubitably, Human Resource Departments just confoundingly ignore the poor managers in Corporate America, and I think part of it is systemic in nature.

The other problem is that the manager's boss plays into the equation as well, and once human resources starts down that road, they are taking on a lot of powerful people who for the most part outrank them in the corporation at the individual case level. It is just so much smoother and easier to blame everything on the problem employee and get rid of them like yesterday's garbage.

I would almost feel sorry for the position that human

resources representatives are put into on a daily basis with the overall lack of managerial oversight by the leadership team and support for their function within the corporation at large. However, in dealing with some of the shortsighted gatekeeping mentality that resides in Human Resources Departments these days, they all knew what they signed up for, and went running to the mediocrity and dysfunctional abyss. It says a lot about the types of individuals who work in Human Resources. And I am not trying to be mean here, just portray an accurate description of your typical Human Resources Department and representative employee base.

Human Resources Departments are completely useless these days, and this is common knowledge among the population in the workplace in Corporate America.

If you have a problem with your manager, you should do your duty as if Human Resources were a competent department that would conduct a thorough investigation into your matter. Document the issue in writing through a very well organized, thought out and thorough manner. And most importantly, present this documented issue to your human resources representative with a very calm, rational, and unemotional approach by means of a face to face meeting. You have done your required sense of corporate duty, reported the issue and documented it for future reference.

But don't expect any meaningful results from this route, as we referenced earlier in the Google example. Oftentimes, Human Resources will not put the necessary work into fully investigating and understanding your documented issue. Additionally, they don't understand the significance or underlying merits of the facts you are laying out in your documentation. And in many cases, just flat out don't care about the facts you documented in your case.

The most likely outcome is that Human Resources will spend more effort sticking to their original belief structure going in that you are a problem employee, and there must be something wrong with you. After all, the benefit of the doubt systematically always goes to the manager in these cases.

Human Resources will literally go out of their way trying to explain away, lessen, rationalize, or outright refute your documented claims than actually investigating them in any great detail. It is a crazy phenomenon regarding belief structures and human nature. There are psychological studies that show people who hold socially, religiously, culturally, and environmentally influenced beliefs will go out of their way to disregard evidence contrary to their original beliefs no matter how strong and credible the evidence.[7]

This phenomenon actually has theoretical underpinnings in some of the philosophy of Willard Van Orman Quine's epistemological work regarding his Web of Belief.[8] In layman's terms, human beings are much more willing to change things they believe on the periphery of their core belief structure, Web of Beliefs, than they are to change things they believe that are central, internal and integral to their core belief structure.[9]

Basically, people hang on tightly to those core beliefs, and you can understand how long ingrained, systemic corporate behavior, beliefs and practices are hard to change once they get a foothold in corporations. I bet you didn't think I would work some philosophy into a conversation about human resources when you picked up this book.

---

[7] https://en.wikipedia.org/wiki/Belief_perseverance; https://www.lifeweavings.org/the-essential-humanity-of-cognitive-dissonance/; https://www.scientificamerican.com/article/how-to-convince-someone-when-facts-fail/

[8] https://plato.stanford.edu/entries/quine/; https://emilkirkegaard.dk/en/wp-content/uploads/W.-V.-Quine-J.-S.-Ullian-The-Web-of-Belief.pdf

[9] https://www.amazon.com/Web-Belief-W-V-Quine/dp/0075536099

3 PIP

In this chapter we are going to discuss the employee Performance Improvement Plan also known as PIP. These employee PIPs can be really detailed, sophisticated legal documents or they can be as simple as a bunch of bullet point notes typed up in a word document. There is a lot of variability in the processes and formal requirements of PIP even at some of the best Fortune 500 companies in the world.

Similar to a great number of things in society, human beings operate with a lot of group think, and consequently certain behaviors and practices get adopted in trend like fashion. PIP sounded like a good idea when it first made the rounds of human resources departments and professionals.

I guess it was sort of like their way of adding value, since most of their power and responsibilities within the corporate structure have been eroded through the years. Thus, anytime they can create some "value-added" to further justify their importance and existence, you know they will jump on it like any bureaucratic appendage in society. Yes, I have an exceptionally low opinion, as do most people in corporations of human resources departments and the people that work in these areas.

The concept isn't so bad if the intent of providing feedback and concrete steps or guidelines to employees who are struggling or underperforming in their role is to help them get back on track, improve in areas, and support them towards the goal of growing as employees in meeting or exceeding expectations in the future.

However, this isn't how PIP is used for the most part. It has become a caricature of its original intent and has been aggressively abused by most managers in the corporate world. The old line about giving people a little information can be a dangerous thing, and power in the wrong hands, or weapons of mass destruction in the wrong hands is just a recipe for disaster.

Given how I have seen PIP handled by managers at the corporate level, I would have loved to sit in on how PIP was presented to them as a tool, the type of guidelines given, and managerial training that went along with their introduction and familiarity with the tool. It would be interesting to see the communication gap between how they were instructed to utilize PIP, and how these managers actually use the tool.

Not that it matters because I have seen rookie managers that were so wet behind the ears that they wouldn't have had time to be trained on any managerial principles, practices, and theory. These people were just thrown into the position without any preparation whatsoever, and six months later they are putting working professionals who have decades of experience on PIP because they had an inclination and impulse to do so thanks to their aha moment of great experiential wisdom.

The truth of the matter is that today in corporations PIP has become so abused that it isn't a tool to help improve employee performance. It isn't even a tool to lay the groundwork for firing an employee, which is one of the purposes of the tool.

The real use of PIP has become so distorted that managers routinely put employees on PIP who they don't like, purely for petty, vindictive agendas of personal payback regarding issues that have nothing to do with actual job performance. In fact, the managers abuse PIP so much that they often have to make up outright lies about the employee just to fill out the document and justify the meeting in the first place.

There isn't an objective process that is followed, no regimented review regarding a PIP event which is conducted on behalf of upper management or some committee in the business unit or corporation at large that oversees the entire PIP process in a non-biased manner.

As a result, managers have learned that there is no accountability in the actual carrying out of the PIP event from their perspective. They can put someone on PIP without any repercussions for whatever reason they want, and for any little petty explanation that their small mindedness and hurt feelings can come up with as a pseudo-justification. A real abuse of power on full display, and why you don't give people tools and power that they are not responsible or professional enough to enact in a thoroughgoing and thoughtful manner in the first place.

Here is how a PIP process usually goes down in a corporation. The manager doesn't like the employee for whatever reason and is looking to put the employee under their foot, step on them a bit, and show them who is boss. The PIP event is really all about control in many cases, and an insecure manager using PIP to establish or reassert dominance with the employee through the PIP process.

This is why the manager doesn't have a meeting with the employee and say, "Well Dave, I am not happy with your performance lately, and if you don't improve in these areas I think are important for the role and this department, then I am going to have to put you on PIP. This is what PIP is, what it entails, and tries to do as a process."

However, managers never tell the employee in this purposeful manner, instead they schedule a meeting just like any other weekly meeting with your boss, and with no mention of PIP on the meeting notice whatsoever, just to get the full "Blindside effect" for the employee who is utterly shocked when there is a human resources person in a conference room who they don't know from Adam, and the manager and the human resources representative gang up on this totally shocked employee who was probably having a great day before this meeting.

Tell me this process is good for company morale, tell me this is trying to improve or motivate the employee to do their job better, tell me this isn't purely about mean-spirited payback, and managerial vindictiveness at its finest in Corporate America.

The funny thing is that the human resources representative just nods her head to everything the incompetent manager is saying, like the human resources representative knows anything substantive about anything involved in the PIP document other than the legal parts that they were trained on. This is the rub, nobody ever verifies anything that is put into a PIP document beforehand, it just gets rubber stamped. If the incompetent manager says it is so, then this becomes fact, no matter how ridiculous the statements or outright lies in the document.

If human resources ever conducted some research into the PIP process, they would realize that there is a strong correlation between incompetent managers and putting employees on PIP in the first place. It says a lot about you as a manager, if you have to put employees on PIP. It says even more when these are experienced professionals who know what they are doing from a work product and responsibility standpoint. The real irony here is that the managers who are routinely putting employees on Performance Improvement Plans, are actually demonstrating their own incompetence as managers, and should probably be the ones being put on PIP to begin with.

At any rate, when an employee is put on PIP, even if everything in the document is complete balderdash, the employee has no realistic and effective recourse available to them because if they try to escalate this to someone higher up in human resources or upper management these people will just take the manager's side.

Remember, most behaviors in corporations are motivated by covering your ass concerns, and since it would be apparent that human resources didn't properly train the manager on how to suitably utilize PIP as a tool, they have to always back the manager, even if the employee has emails or documents that contradict accounts that are regularly misstated in a PIP document. It really doesn't matter in most circumstances as it will all be explained away by the manager, and human resources without fail, always has the back of the manager.

You can go to the manager's boss, but you better believe they have the manager's back. After all, I am sure the manager acts completely differently around their manager and spends a lot of time nurturing their relationship. Thus, they may say some impartial things, but in the end they will always side with the manager. What is really going on behind the scenes here is that they are all members of the same affiliated club, the "Us and Them" club, the club of managers.

You are just viewed as some rank and file employee who basically has no rights, you belong to the working group level club. Employees at the working group level are viewed as easily replaceable and second-class citizens despite what human resources or upper management says to the contrary at town hall meetings or in ridiculously produced corporate propaganda videos discussing some balderdash vis-à-vis company values and valuing all employees the same.

You can try to escalate this several levels above your manager's boss, and although they might meet with you, if you word the email in such a way where they realize they better meet with you to make sure they are covering their ass. This meeting is largely for show, and nothing beneficial for your case will come from this meeting. Let me remind the reader that I am not telling you how things should work in principle, but rather how they actually work in practice at corporations.

You simply look like a disgruntled problem employee who just got put on PIP and is now complaining to them about it. The meeting cannot end fast enough for this big boss, who will just steer the conversation away from your legitimate issues and try their best to minimalize and trivialize everything that is a serious discussion point regarding your case. The big boss may make a couple of perfunctory notes while you are speaking, but in the end, they will be supporting the entire nonsensical and unwarranted PIP procedure.

Another point to be made here is that corporations never take a PIP back once it has been handed out to an employee. So the big boss can write copious notes on their little notepad while you are making your case, and even if you prove that everything in the PIP document is patently false, you are still being put on PIP.

This is part of the lunacy that is rampant in Corporate America, even if you have proven that you shouldn't have been put on PIP, according to the very arguments put forth and stated in the PIP document, you are still being put on PIP. It is like once the PIP process gets started, it must proceed to fruition no matter what!

The reasoning here is that it makes everyone in the corporation look bad from your manager to human resources and upper management if they start taking back PIPs through an adjudicated process. Best to just rubber stamp these indiscriminately and avoid the embarrassing PIP miscues along the way. What kind of malarkey process is this for corporations? Yes, you got it, it's complete hogwash to say the least!

So until human resources and corporate management comes to the realization that managers do not have the skillset or mental aptitude to properly hand out or manage the PIP process and take this all away. Until this day comes, which of course, will be ten years too late. This just represents the snail's pace of change in Corporate America these days. Just go online and read the PIP horror stories on how badly the entire PIP process is applied and carried out at the best corporations in the world of business, and you will start to get a sense of the entire absurdity and failure that PIP embodies in corroding the corporate workplace with visceral and endemic animosity.

But until this day of reason comes in Corporate America, just know that you can be put on PIP for a multitude of pretexts that have truly little to do with job performance. You can be put on PIP for something as stupid as making a funny smirk when your manager discusses a project you are working on, you roll your eyes slightly in a meeting with team members, or you just don't get along that well with your boss.

You can be put on PIP because the manager just hates the way you express yourself, your political and social affiliations, or simply because of your overall appearance and demeanor. Fundamentally, you can be put on PIP for anything that happens to irritate some incompetent, insecure, and petty manager, and there are plenty of those in Corporate America, just simply out of the blue with no notice whatsoever.

So expect this as a potential landmine in the corporate world. This is why you are reading this book, to learn things about the corporate world you didn't know or wouldn't have personally experienced before in the workplace.

First and foremost, always keep your cool, no matter what your boss says during the proceedings. This of course assumes you haven't already fainted and require medical attention in getting over the shock of being totally blindsided by the PIP process in the first place.

Be very polite, nod your head in an extremely cooperative manner, and maintain a positive and open body posture at all times. Moreover, be reassuring that what your manager is saying during this process is the absolute gospel, that you will work with them to improve your performance and work tirelessly through the PIP process in a conscientious manner.

This is the only way to play the PIP game from an optimal theory standpoint. The polite, calm level-headed approach where you demonstrate that you are eager to work through the process and improve as an employee does a couple of beneficial things as a strategy. It shows you under the best light possible given the tense and difficult circumstances of you being put on PIP, and it runs contrary to what is in the document because a poor problem employee wouldn't react this way to being completely blindsided by a PIP meeting.

If you lose your cool, raise your voice, argue with the manager, you just end up validating everything in the PIP document. In fact, your boss will say to the human resources representative after the meeting, "See, I told you Lisa has attitude problems!" You fit the problem employee as described in the PIP document by objecting in any aspect or getting angry in any fashion during the PIP meeting with your manager and the human resources representative.

The real irony is that if these are a bunch of balderdash lies on behalf of the manager or half-truths that don't deserve a PIP action, it is perfectly reasonable for the employee to be upset after being blindsided by an incompetent boss during a PIP meeting.

But this isn't how it will be viewed by human resources and your manager; it serves as just another instance of your insubordination as a problem employee. Hence, the entire PIP process becomes self-fulfilling and is never actually vetted by an objective and non-biased committee. In reality, Performance Improvement Plans are handed out like candy at Halloween and reflect a process that is completely abused by most managers in the corporate world.

After you get out of the PIP meeting, and you have been the perfect little punching bag, start looking for your next job in all of your free time. The goal is to extend the PIP process for as long as possible until you can find another good job.

Hopefully one with a much better manager because you never want to work for a manager who would blindside a coveted employee and a valued member of their team with a PIP process meeting out of left field.

This is a real meanspirited, vindictive manager, and you want to get far away from these types of managers in the corporate world. But unfortunately, in today's tight labor market there are a lot of incompetent, highly vindictive and meanspirited managers out there in Corporate America.

4 ALWAYS KEEP YOUR COOL

In this chapter we discuss keeping your cool. Anyone can keep their cool when things are going well, unless they are a real hothead or mentally unbalanced. But it is considerably more difficult for even well-balanced people to keep their cool when things are going poorly.

However, the final case is one where something so extraordinary happens that even the most laid back and calm person would be reasonably expected to lose their cool in the situation. In fact, it would be unreasonable and not normal for this person to be able to keep their cool under these extraordinary circumstances.

It is precisely this final case where you need to be prepared for learning how to keep your cool by going against your natural inclinations. It is this extraordinary circumstance where it is perfectly reasonable for you to get upset and lose your cool that you need to train your mind to avoid losing your cool.

You unequivocally always lose when you get emotional in a corporate setting and lose your cool. Your arguments become jumbled, you end up rushing your words, listeners start focusing on your emotional state and become distracted by your physical mannerisms. They mentally take note of the fact that you are losing your cool, and they aren't paying attention to what you are actually saying anymore.

Human beings in a corporate setting at a Fortune 500 company are some of the most educated, well rounded, and socially adjusted individuals on the planet. They are experienced in consistently having rational, multi-faceted and successful conversations under all kinds of differing and complex environments.

However, all employees have egos and expectations for what they believe is fair, customary, and acceptable practices both from society at large in their everyday interactions, and specifically in the course of their working relationships at the office.

It is when things happen at work that fall outside their expectations regarding normal behavior and fair treatment where they become upset and ultimately lose their cool. In some sense, employees let their guard down and expect higher standards regarding behavioral norms at corporations than they do in other social settings they routinely encounter like grocery shopping or attending a sporting event.

After all, corporations spend so much time promoting their corporate values, and are always putting the best face on everything at the office, that employees may actually start to feel secure at the workplace, a sort of safe zone from the bad behaviors of the outside world. Well, this just isn't the case, as corporations represent a microcosm of society at large, and the same reasons for conflicts in the outside world, also exist inside the walls of Fortune 500 companies.

You need to prepare yourself as an employee for the most ridiculous, straight out of left field behaviors, inappropriate treatment, unfair practices, and downright dirty deeds that you can only imagine in your worst-case scenarios. This way you will never be naively shocked, have your expectations blasted to smithereens, and you will never be surprised or caught off guard to the point of losing your cool.

Remember, this is all a game. Just keep that mindset in your thoughts at all times, and you will approach difficult and hostile situations much better prepared, with an enthusiastic, confident, and professional smile on your face and remain cool as a cucumber.

As trust me you are going to encounter bullying at the office, total disrespect of you as a person, snide comments, completely inappropriate and unprofessional behavior, and experience really unfair practices and poor treatment sometime during your career in the corporate world. And probably multiple times during your corporate career, through diverse sets of unexpected circumstances with colleagues who you have every reasonable right to lose your cool in reaction to their deplorable behaviors.

But these areas are where you lose twice. The first is the inappropriate treatment, and the second is you losing your cool. Just ask yourself, do you like the feeling you get when you lose your cool. Does this mental state feel good, are you having fun, is this mental state good for your blood pressure, stress levels and overall health? This is what I mean by losing a second time, your reaction in losing your cool, is your second loss in the office transaction. Furthermore, you are also inevitably making the problem worse for yourself because you now have additionally lost your cool on top of the original problem.

Consequently, keep your cool at all times, no matter the circumstances. Expect to get backstabbed by a co-worker, lied about by a colleague, thrown under the bus for something you didn't do, verbally abused, intimidated by your boss, physically threatened, treated unfairly, sabotaged on a project you are working, criticized regularly, and routinely maligned by a group of resentful coworkers behind your back. Moreover, at some jobs, this can all happen before lunch on Monday of the working week!

There are certainly worse behaviors than these, but most

employees are not even prepared to handle these types of encounters at the office, and become highly stressed out, visibly upset, and ultimately lose their respective cool.

Sure you can follow the proper reporting procedures in some cases to address certain types of inappropriate encounters and unprofessional interactions at work, but you weaken your credibility if you lose your cool at any time during the process. And moreover, don't expect human resources to be your savior, or by escalating a problem to upper management that this will resolve the issue in a fair manner. Oftentimes, human resources and upper management are completely useless as resources for these types of conflict resolution issues you encounter at the office.

What's the old adage, if you have to go to human resources to report a problem, you might as well start looking to find a new job. Sure, if you have an easy open and shut case where your boss yelled inappropriate things at you in front of a bunch of witnesses, then by all means go to human resources as they will be able to effectively handle these types of cases.

However, you will find that there will always be these nuanced subtle conflict scenarios that happen in corporations where human resources will ultimately side with the more powerful person the majority of the time. Alternatively, human resources will just spin the issue to make it less onerous, or just have a bunch of useless discussions and meetings that accomplish extraordinarily little and only make the situation worse. Sometimes human resources will simply provide cursory lip service to your problems, and secretly believe that you are either high maintenance or a problem employee.

The same goes for escalating many issues to upper management, they will say all the right things, usually diffuse the importance and severity of the issues, and ultimately think to themselves, "Why is this person in my office." They really don't care about your little issue; their biggest concern is "CYA" covering their ass in this process and making sure this little headache of an issue doesn't personally stick to them in any manner. If they can pass the issue on to someone else without anything sticking to them, the more the better in these cases. They will of course say all the right things, spew out some corporate marketing gibberish, write a few notes down on paper, but in all likelihood will not have your back at all.

These people aren't sticking their neck out for anybody, and ironically this behavior often gets them in trouble when an issue really blows up at the company. This usually happens when a full-blown investigation shows that the issue was brought to their attention and they failed to adequately address the issue. Instead, upper management just tried to sweep the issue or problem under the rug so to speak.

In other words, expect to be disappointed a lot at the office in Corporate America. And expect to really be challenged with your ability to maintain your cool at all times in the office. Always keep in mind, this is all a game, and the best way to play it is by keeping your emotions in check even under the most hostile and unreasonable situations at the office.

In fact, sometimes your colleagues are purposefully trying to push buttons. They are deliberately misstating the facts or situations to try and provoke you to lose your cool because they realize that they win the game by getting you to lose your cool. You always look worse under any situation by losing your cool, especially at Fortune 500 corporations where professional etiquette is expected, promoted, and held in such high regard.

Once you publicly lose your cool or become visibly angry you look like the irrational, out of control, problem personality at the office. And like I stated previously, in many cases it would be perfectly reasonable for you to become upset, angry and lose your cool at the office. This is what makes it so hard to control because in many cases you have to act irrationally to avoid losing your cool. As the rational, natural human response would be to lose your cool in many cases.

The basis for PIP being one of the recurrent themes in this book is that it has become the default mechanism or behavioral enforcement tool to mete out cruel and inconsiderate punishment, make arbitrary judgments about employees, carry out personal vendettas against people, subjectively force rank employees, motivate and pressure workers to quit, and ultimately lay the groundwork for justified and sanctioned firings at corporations.

The PIP instrument is effectively death row and the electric chair of the corporate world, so much so, that corporations should give employees a special last meal of their choice before being executed via the PIP process. The wonderous creation of PIP really has evolved into one nasty mechanism of behavioral and social control which represents the ultimate power play against rank and file employees in Corporate America.

Let me provide the following scenario to illustrate the point. You have your weekly scheduled meeting with your boss, you check the meeting room on your office calendar, show up early and your boss and a human resources representative are already sitting there on the other side of the conference table with smug little gotcha smirks on their faces.

You thought this was just your weekly scheduled meeting with your boss. In fact, your snake boss gave no indications that anything special was taking place in this meeting beforehand, so you are completely blindsided when this is actually a PIP action meeting instead.

You are thinking that everything is going great in your new job, you are meeting all of your work deadlines, completing all of your assigned project deliverables, and thinking positive thoughts about the course of your career at the company. And all the sudden you are being blindsided in a PIP meeting where your boss is outright making up stuff about your performance, lying to your face about your record, and seems like an entirely different person.

This is the first time you are hearing any of this stuff from your snake boss who you now believe is actually *The Devil incarnate*. Under this scenario it is going to be rather difficult to keep your cool and not become visibly angry with this workplace injustice happening right before you in real time.

It would be perfectly reasonable for you to lose your cool under the circumstances, especially if these are really meanspirited, and outright false claims that aren't remotely close to approximating reality even in some parallel universe, and your boss has effectively lost their freaking mind.

Well this very scenario happens all the time in Corporate America, and there are a lot of vindictive, mean-spirited bosses that will completely lie about your overall record and job performance. They will blame you for something you didn't do.

These snake bosses will put you on PIP for a myriad of reasons that have nothing to do with what PIP was actually designed for just because they can. And many times it is to take the heat off of their own poor performance or to save their management record by blaming you for something they caused in the first place or throw you under the bus to make you the departmental scapegoat.

These are the types of nasty games that routinely occur in Corporate America, and human resources or upper management isn't going to be your savior and come riding to your rescue in most cases.

However, if you compound matters by losing your cool during this process, you just end up validating all the untruths and worst impressions that human resources or upper management have been given by your snake boss in their attempt to damage your career, hurt your reputation and throw you under the bus.

Losing your cool, makes you seem like the bad person or guilty party in the process. Once you lose your collective cool, you have already lost the corporate game.

Your boss is actually trying to get you to lose your cool, it gives their case more credibility in the end. Learn how to play the game, and never lose your cool, regardless of the situation.

I don't care if your snake boss is saying outright lies in front of upper management and human resources, they are accusing you of various infractions and mistakes that are patently false, and they are physically slapping your face twice just for the fun of it.

Just take it all in, smile on the inside, and recognize that you are playing the game perfectly by not losing your cool even under the most extreme scenarios. Just maintain your Zen-like calm demeanor at all times, and you will be well on your way to winning this corporate game.

This actually gives you more credibility because human resources and upper management will be impressed with your composure level and how well you play the game.

They can really use this type of person in their organization because this skillset is so rare in this world at large and in the corporate world specifically. Most people cannot keep their cool in unreasonable conflict scenarios, and those that can remain calm score additional points in the eyes of their colleagues.

As make no mistake, upper management people have all realized by this point in their careers that this is all a game. They have become good game players themselves or they would never have gotten this far up the corporate ladder. The higher up you get, the better you become at playing the corporate game. You become good at recognizing all the potential traps and learn how to avoid the typical landmines that take out many a poor game player at the corporate level.

In fact, if you ever listen closely to a corporate executive, they are the master of corporate gibberish. These executives are the masters of trite little corporate buzzwords and nonsensical speech that sounds great but doesn't actually say or commit to anything.

This corporate speak is just a bunch of balderdash that accomplishes the goals of diversion, deflection, corporate spinning, and creative marketing. These corporate executives' primary objective is always to promote themselves while CYA covering their ass at all times.

This corporate nonsensical gibberish is quite an effective and necessary tool for any expert game player that rises high in the corporate hierarchy.

In summary, just remember that when you lose your cool at the office, you end up losing twice in the workplace transaction. You lose the first time by getting screwed at the office, and you lose the second time by your poor reaction to getting screwed at the office. Losing your cool to getting screwed at the office only makes the situation worse.

You have to learn how to always keep your cool at the office, and it is an essential life tool outside the office as well. Think in terms of the tennis player that always keeps their cool no matter what chaotic events are occurring around them. This tennis player is playing the game with the optimal game theory mindset.

5 COMPETENCY DOESN'T MATTER

In this chapter we will discuss competency and why this isn't the holy grail to avoid being brought down by corporate politics. You might think to yourself that the underperformers are the ones that fall prey to the game of office politics. Sort of like how the weak ones are picked on in school or lions look for the unhealthy and feeble behaving animals in a herd of wildebeest. Sure there is some of this that occurs in corporate settings, but competent people have their own troubles in the harsh corporate environment as well.

The reason why competent people are targets in Corporate America is that most people in corporations are average to really bad at their jobs. In fact, it is a wonder anything gets done at all in corporations these days with all the incompetent people being employed who are not qualified or capable of doing the core responsibilities of their roles. You might think to yourself right now that it cannot be that bad, when in fact it is even worse than you can possibly imagine at most corporations in America.

The only things that consistently get done at corporations these days are the basic necessities that have to be completed to keep the operations running at a minimum level. The lowest of the low hanging fruit is what gets tackled and completed at corporations today. Just forget about the high-level, value-added projects being tackled. These are viewed as luxury items in Corporate

America that usually get sidetracked and delayed quarter after quarter for most companies.

There is extraordinarily little smart sourcing taking place at most corporations, forget about system upgrades that streamline obsolete and inefficient practices or proactive planning for the future business needs of the company. There is only minimal market intelligence and negligible data analysis taking place at corporations that confers any real competitive advantage for making well-informed and smarter business decisions.

I have worked and consulted with the best Fortune 500 companies in America, and most of these business units have no handle on the implications of their spend data, how badly they misappropriate capital, and why they cannot properly forecast their future business needs. I have colleagues that work on the inside of some of the best companies in America, and the stories of what routinely goes on every year in these companies is frankly shocking.

I am talking about software projects meant to update all of the previous legacy software systems by integrating the entire company on a new modern software system that fails so badly that the corporation is forced to go back to the previous legacy software systems. This very example is so common a problem for corporations that it is repeated at company after company in the United States.

If we are talking about spend analysis, I can tell you that the best procurement departments at Fortune 500 corporations really are clueless regarding their spend data. Good luck even coming up with a spend number that everyone agrees is the right one to use in making important business decisions and annual comparisons.

The spend numbers that they do come up with are usually all over the place, and due to system constraints from a data collection, running reports and overall reporting standpoint, companies usually have several spend numbers that they use for different purposes.

It is interesting that in the age of data analytics, advanced metrics, real-time market intelligence and smart computer programming, most corporations lack the competent people and accurate up-to-date software systems to properly analyze all the data at their disposal.

This is why most corporations employ consultants to try and fill in the competency gaps where they are routinely dropping the ball. There is truly little competency in Corporate America, think in terms of the glory days of US auto manufacturing, consumer electronics, airline travel and great corporations.

There is an appreciable reason the German automobile companies eat America's lunch, Korean electronics companies are making all our appliances these days, and most of the products on Amazon come from other countries.

America is a second-rate country that is on the downswing from a competitive standpoint. Moreover, America's educational system is not competitive by world standards and we have become lazy with noticeably short attention spans as a culture.

We produce extraordinarily little of value these days outside of the entertainment field, and most of that is complete garbage compared to the glory days of the studio system where quality productions were the norm.

So trust me when I say this competency gap in Corporate America stands out like a black swan these days, and when it is present, it makes everybody else look particularly bad. Everyone badmouths and gossips and says negative things about the competent person in the office, "Look at Jim trying to get all this work done, he has created all this extra work for my department and team members, can you believe his requests?"

Honestly, if you want to fit right in with Corporate America, then do the basic minimum that is required of your position. Spend the majority of the time talking to your boss about their kids and taking a special interest in their lives.

Your number one goal is to make your direct boss happy, and that they feel extremely comfortable interacting with you on the job. Go have a beer with them after work on Fridays. Play golf and tennis or hunt with them on the weekends with the goal of becoming their best friend at the office.

Take an interest in their problems, talk about their favorite hobbies, and discuss the subjects they like talking the most about during their free time. All this superficial stuff is actually much more important than truly going the extra mile in getting the work done in many cases.

I am not telling you that getting your work done isn't important. I am just trying to illustrate the point that personality and attitude are the most important characteristic or deciding factor for your success in an incompetent oriented workplace environment.

Just look around your company and you will notice many people who don't ever accomplish anything. These people are put in charge of projects that always fail, are routinely behind schedule, and they never accomplish anything of value or substance at the office.

But these same people have managed to keep a good job by just sort of blending into the office furniture. They don't make any waves at the office in a purposeful manner as a sort of camouflaging incompetence strategy. They usually have a good personable communication style and accomplish absolutely nothing at work year after year.

Meanwhile some hard charging ambitious person who is trying to get things done makes all kinds of enemies at the office. In fact, everyone secretly hates this person and is extremely jealous of their work ethic and accomplishments at the office, "Who does Jeffrey think he is, anyway?"

This person doesn't stand a chance of working for very long at this corporation because somebody will find a way to sabotage them on a project or throw them under the bus for something. Just mark my word, it happens all the time in the corporate world.

So the point here is that personal style is much more important than actual competency. Just pay attention and learn from the office culture, what type of personal style or work characteristic is rewarded or punished at your company?

Now if your boss already hates your guts, and you have lost the battle of trying to be friends, and there is no chance in hell to have your boss actually like you as an employee or person. In this case, then you better work your ass off because any little mistake will be well documented in an effort to make an example of you for the rank and file.

They will also punish you in a number of ways strictly because they don't like you and this may include being removed from the company. In short, if your boss doesn't like you, then you will have to work twice as hard to make them happy and keep them off your back!

This means anytime the boss can step on you and put you in your place is fair game in their minds. There are many bosses out there in Corporate America who are just waiting for you to make a mistake so they can step on you like a bug.

These corporate psychopaths want to twist their proverbial shoe into your chest and grind your soul down into the corporate carpet with such malicious intent and joyous satisfaction that you will be begging for mercy.

Once your boss has reached the stage of hating your guts, it is time to find a new job as soon as possible, as they will find fault with anything and everything while making your time there a living hell.

In this scenario, you need to be looking for another job and take the abuse without being confrontational or losing your cool. Just play the game here and recognize that you are playing the game perfectly from an optimal strategy and game theory standpoint.

Don't let your ego get involved and avoid making these office dramas personal. The office adversaries want you to get mad. They would like for you to lose your cool and become confrontational while they remain calm and detached corporate game players. And remember you lose twice under this scenario.

There are a lot of incompetent and mean-spirited bosses out there in the corporate world, however, you are equally responsible in how you react to their stupidity. You lose the first time by having a mean-spirited and terrible boss, and you lose the second time by getting frustrated and losing your cool in response to this horrible boss. Now you have displayed a bad attitude that everyone in the office can witness firsthand.

Don't worry about the mean-spirited and incompetent bosses, just keep your cool, continue to play the game, and give these bosses just enough rope to hang themselves. These people eventually self-destruct and end up destroying their corporate careers through sheer stupidity, incompetence, and poor behavior.

Just don't let them take you down before they self-destruct by reacting poorly to their actions. If you lose your cool, then you have reacted poorly to their actions. This is just how the corporate game is played.

You have to astutely recognize this as the game that it is, and the best strategy is to play the game with a Zen-like calmness and analytical mindset. You should be smiling on the inside whilst your boss is the one losing their respective cool because you are outplaying them in this corporate game.

6 THE BOSS IS YOUR ONLY PRIORITY

In this chapter we discuss keeping your boss happy, as everyone at a Fortune 500 company has a boss, including the CEO who has major shareholders and the board of directors to keep in their good graces.

Many employees think that if they just do all their work on time, show up each day ready to work, and do everything expected of them at the office that they are secure in their job from a performance evaluation standpoint.

In fact, many employees realize that they might be having specific clashes with their boss on how to approach a project, and the types of training classes they can sign up for at work. There might also be clashes regarding when they can go on vacation, and in prioritizing requests which come from outside their corresponding business unit. These are just slight little clashes which demonstrate the fact that you and your boss don't mesh perfectly, and that there is some underlying tension present in the relationship.

This isn't unusual with boss-employee relationships; however most employees think they can just ignore this tension, do their work and everything will be fine. This just isn't the case, and this is the wrong approach to take in thinking about your boss relationship.

Undoubtedly there are bosses and managers that aren't petty and are very sophisticated individuals who are secure with themselves and have great people skills. There are bosses who don't take things personally and recognize that they don't have to agree on every single point with their employees in order to have effective relationships that get the required work done for the company.

But there are a lot of bosses and managers who internalize everything. These managers take every little disagreement, however insignificant and blow it up in their minds. The direct reports for these managers are always walking on eggshells because everything is routinely blown out of proportion. In short, these managers take everything personally.

As a matter of fact, you never want to have any disagreements with these managers. Moreover, you can forget about stating your opinion or preferences on projects in any way. In these cases, clashing with your boss, even on minor details will be viewed as an act of insubordination towards their authority. This is a big deal for these insecure, domineering bosses and voicing your opinion in any way is tantamount to a declaration of war in their minds.

The ignoring the problem and hoping that it will just go away strategy will get you put on PIP or fired from the company faster than you can say, "What about my rights?" And it doesn't matter that you have only been with the company or in your new position for a short period of time.

When you are starting to clash with your manager or boss on even small things, this is your wake-up call to change the way in which you communicate and interact with your boss. I realize that some bosses are exceedingly difficult people to work for, but in the corporate world of reality it doesn't matter, your boss or manager is always right.

I realize this goes against what corporate gobbledygook communications will say regarding voicing your concerns at the company, and all the "Office Correct" corporate platitudes put out by human resources. But in reality, nobody will have your back when you go to human resources or speak to other relevant people in the organization about your manager's difficult personality. So it is a moot point! Remember I am here to tell you how things really are in Corporate America, not how we would like things to be, or how things should be done in the corporate workplace.

All those people who will give you the same corporate balderdash about company values or freedom to speak up regarding your concerns are hypocrites because these same people will not have your back when you do the very things they discuss and promote publicly for appearances' sake.

Yeah you guessed correctly, this is all part of the game playing that goes on in the corporate world, people say one thing, but they do the exact opposite in practice. This is really all about one of the most important principles in Corporate America, always "CYA" cover your ass, which dominates corporate relationships and behaviors at all levels of the corporation.

As A Result, I don't care how difficult your boss is to work with, do not have disagreements or clashes with your boss. It is best to have the mentality that your boss or manager is always right, and whatever they want or desire, you are there to serve. Let someone else on the team raise their concerns, voice their opinions, and report your boss to human resources or upper management. Let these colleagues get on the manager's bad side and official hit list. Let these gluttons for punishment be departmental heroes or sacrificial lambs that take one for the team.

Yes, I recognize this strategy goes against everything you have been taught since grade school about speaking up when you see something that you think is wrong, and that you should be actively reporting bad behavior. Just keep in mind that bad behavior goes on every day in Corporate America, and most of these people still have their jobs despite the poor conduct.

I am sure every single CEO, manager and human

resources representative will swear up and down that this is false, and that they actually encourage people to speak up at the office and voice their concerns. However, this is complete corporate malarkey. Corporate people are so full of balderdash, as two-faced as a vaudevillian comedian, and are always in the covering their ass mode. Therefore, it is wise to take everything you hear at the office from the leadership team with a huge grain of salt. These people are usually just talking their book so to speak.

Do you want to keep your job? Do you realize how hard it is to find a good job at a Fortune 500 company? Just think about all the time spent job hunting, going on interviews, taking drug tests, completing psychological assessments, and filling out all those ridiculously repetitive employment applications online. It's just a huge time commitment which you probably have downplayed in your mind because you now have a job and have forgotten all the hoops you had to jump through in getting the job.

So the moral of the story is that you don't gamble or take chances with your corporate career. You don't clash with your boss or manager on anything, period. What they say is gospel at all times! This of course, assumes that they are not cooking the books, breaking the law, and murdering someone at the office.

Let some colleagues be stupid or naïve enough to buy into the corporate doubletalk and gibberish about taking a principled stand against their boss. Let these suicide pilots take their disagreements with their managers to human resources or escalate matters all the way up the corporate food chain to the big boss and watch how far that gets them in the corporate world.

Unless everyone hates this manager and upper management is just looking for an excuse to drop the hammer on them, then most of the relevant people that count will have the manager's back in any dispute. Moreover, I am sure the manager is actually nice to all the relevant people that count in the corporation. The manager is keeping these people happy because they understand the rules of the game and keeping these important people happy is always in their best interest. Thus, none of the relevant people worth consulting in an office dispute with the manager will have the employee's back who takes the issue outside the department.

This is the difference between how things are said to be done, and how they are actually done in a corporate setting. Sure there are always exceptions to this rule, but we aren't basing a coherent game playing strategy on exceptions. We are simply building a strategy around the base case scenario.

In some cases you can benefit when a fellow team member takes one for the department and reports your mean-spirited boss or manager. This is the ideal scenario because all the sudden your boss will be on their best behavior towards their direct reports. However, your fellow team member is on borrowed time with this corporation and should start looking for another job immediately. Even if the boss was reprimanded for poor behavior, this boss will carry a sizable grudge against the employee for reporting the issue. The mean-spirited boss will work behind the scenes to build alliances to sabotage the employee's career at the corporation.

It should also be pointed out that human resources and the rest of management now view this individual as a problem employee because they make waves, cannot get along with people in the organization, and go running to human resources every time they have disagreements with their boss. Whether this is right or compatible with the corporate values espoused by upper management, the corporation as a living organism always protects itself first and foremost, and the corporate caretakers all hate employees who make waves and cause problems which disrupts the normal flow of business operations.

They won't say this publicly, but nobody likes a snitch, period. I realize that snitch is a rather strong word here, and more at home in a crime drama than a corporate environment, but that is how the corporate caretakers view employees who create problems for the organization.

In fact, having employees routinely being proactive in voicing their concerns regarding the way they are treated "unfairly" by their respective managers is often seen as an existential threat to the company. It is best to nip this type of behavior in the bud before it takes shape and flowers within the psyches of the rank and file employees.

The thinking goes along the lines that pretty soon the inmates will be running the asylum at the corporation. Moreover, the feeling is that this gives too much power to the rank and file employees, and this power grab is at the expense of upper management. This all becomes a rather slippery slope which most corporations wish to avoid entirely or at least minimize as much as possible.

The rationale is simple, people are self-interested beings, and they see the conflict through the eyes of their fellow management colleague. As a result, they identify and side with the manager versus the rank and file employee. They think subconsciously that this could happen to them in the future, and the managers being the corporate caretakers that they are, all take this as an affront to their authority as managers to dictate to employees what they want done.

There have been studies conducted showing that people care about and relate more towards other people's concerns when they are similar to their own.[10] Thus, the one percent have a real problem relating to pretty much anybody on the planet except those in the one percent category.[11]

Managers relate much more towards other managers and not to the concerns and problems of the rank and file

---

[10] https://www.simplypsychology.org/social-identity-theory.html
[11] https://www.wired.com/story/why-are-rich-people-so-mean/

employees. In fact, many managers secretly despise their direct reports, and view them as loyal subjects to be ruled with an iron fist. As a result, they routinely adopt the "Us" and "Them" mentality in regard to their behaviors and interactions with the rank and file employees.

In their minds, managers belong in one group, while rank and file employees belong in a distinct and lower-ranking subordinate group. This is why managers usually act, think and vote as a group in the corporation which indubitably means taking the side of the manager in any dispute with an employee. The employee just comes across as a problem employee who is not a good team player and probably not long for the organization anyway.

Just keep in the back of your mind that there is this power structure that exists in corporations between management and employees. Once you join the club of managers, just like with police officers, there is an unwritten rule that it is always Us and Them. Furthermore, as a card-carrying member of the management club, corporate managers always have the backs of other managers when it comes time to choose sides in a corporate dispute.

The bottom line is that emotional responses and impulsive, ego-driven decision-making leads to bad outcomes at the office. Trust me on this point as I have seen this play out enough times in Corporate America to know the correct way to play the game. Always keep your boss happy regardless of how difficult they are to work with on a daily basis. Just check your ego at the door and don't take any of this personal. This is just the cost of doing business in the corporate world.

You are there to serve your boss and make their job easier in any way possible. It will help if you think about the big picture in all of this which is to successfully advance your corporate career in a strategic fashion. Just remind yourself when you are taking a lot of idiocy from your boss that this is playing the game with the correct strategy. There is nothing to get personally upset about regarding your boss, and don't take anything they may say or do personally, like it is some mortal hit on your self-worth as a human being. Just suck it up, smile politely and play the damn game better than your boss.

In fact, your boss probably wants you to take things personally, but don't give them the satisfaction. One thing I am certain of is that corporate bosses sure don't want you to report them to human resources or upper management, and this is not going to make things better with your boss anyway. Moreover, this isn't the best way to play the corporate game.

Similarly, ignoring the problem with your boss will not make it go away, and one way or another your clashes and disagreements with the boss will be negatively reflected in your employment record. This will happen through poor performance reviews, being put on PIP, and eventually being removed from the company.

In Reality making your boss happy is even more important than doing your work duties, as everything in the office really comes down to how people feel and interact with each other from a relationship standpoint. I know this sounds crazy, but it's true. I have witnessed the most lazy, dawdling, and incompetent employees who accomplish zilch at the office get along just fine in their positions. These people survive year after year with no accountability for their poor performance at work because they have great relationships with their bosses and managers.

These people often have something real important in common with their bosses and they typically have a great interacting style about themselves where their managers just let them slide on everything at the office. Everyone else would have been severely reprimanded, put on PIP or fired a long time ago. Having an amiable communication style and likable personality can truly make up for a lot of skillset inadequacies and poor performance at most corporations.

This isn't the case at companies where performance is the only thing that matters, and ironically these companies often encourage disagreements. The reasoning here is that these companies don't really care if the employees hate each other's guts so long as they produce excellent work product and superior results.

Some examples of companies that put a premium on performance above almost everything else are hedge funds and investment banks. In these companies making money and producing exceptional results is more important than relationship building for the sake of relationship building, and all the other behavioral interaction stuff that regularly plays out in office politics.

This attitude often leads to other problems for these companies though, such as crossing legal and regulatory lines and pushing small edges which often have huge underlying risks associated with them. These behaviors frequently occur because there is such a premium put on the end results of making money for themselves and clients.

The point here is that at some companies, performance overrides the soft skills and personal relationships stuff that predominates at so many Fortune 500 companies. Just know what type of firm you work at, what gets rewarded and punished at the office, to properly understand what rules apply to the corporate game you are playing.

It should be understood that I am not extolling the virtues of being lazy, incompetent, slow to get your work done, and an obsequiously minded corporate sycophant. And I might add that these lazy, incompetent, and underperforming employees are never going to create much value or accomplish anything important during their corporate careers.

These people are not to be emulated or admired in Corporate America. They just serve as an example to illustrate the point that there is a whole lot more to playing the corporate game than working hard and performing quality work at the office. Moreover, making your boss happy is more important than many employees realize and often overrides your actual work product.

So don't think you are too good and above playing the corporate game because you work really hard and produce quality work. Unfortunately, this isn't enough in the wonderful world of corporate politics these days. You have to have a good relationship with your boss, even if this requires a healthy dose of playacting on your part. Just suck it up, put on your stage makeup and play the damn role.

The boss will be none the wiser, and realistically speaking, doesn't even care so long as you respectfully serve their every need in a dutifully loyal manner. In dutifully loyal terms, we are talking about Dog level devotion to your boss here. Accomplish this feat, and your stress levels will be much lower at the office, you will never lose any sleep at night worrying about your terrible relationship with your difficult boss, and your corporate career will be proceeding nicely towards your goals.

The bigger picture here is not letting clashes with an idiot boss or terrible manager get in the way of your corporate career. In fact, your boss or manager may not even be with the company in two to five years, so the goal is to persevere and outlast your difficult manager. Yes, unfortunately there are a lot of really bad managers out there in the corporate world, and you just have to appease them, do whatever it takes to keep them happy, and avoid having them derail your career advancement in any way.

However, don't expect fairness at the office, as nothing is fair in Corporate America. Let me repeat this because it goes against everything that we have been taught growing up in this country, namely, that there is some universal sense of fairness in the world. Well, I can tell you that nothing is fair in Corporate America! In fully grasping this concept and taking it to heart, this will definitely help reduce some naivete and overly optimistic expectations that many corporate employees have regarding the role that fairness plays in determining corporate behaviors and outcomes.

In reality, good hard-working people get fired every day, and complete idiots, corporate sycophants, highly unethical, incompetent, mean-spirited, and unprofessional people routinely get promoted and advance up the corporate ladder. The one thing these people all have in common is that they know how to play the corporate game. Moreover, all these people have been making their bosses happy throughout their snaky and resourceful rise up the corporate ladder.

So just examine your relationship with the boss, if it isn't perfect and you know it needs some work, then think about various ways that you can improve this relationship. It is well worth the investment, even though it may seem like a daunting task at the beginning of this process. The boss is a human being, and deep down, they may not admit it, but they want to be liked and feel loved in their relationships. Find areas where you can bring about these positive feelings in your interactions with the boss. The boss needs to look forward to speaking with you each day at the office.

If you are having infrequent communications with your manager or you go out of your way to avoid speaking with the boss, then this is a huge red flag. So unless your manager or boss travels a lot, has an enormous number of direct reports and a mountain of responsibilities, not speaking frequently with your corporate overlord is usually a very bad sign. You need to have good communications that occur frequently and are continually reinforcing the positive relationship with your feudal lord.

The old saying extolling the virtues of a happy wife leading to a happy life goes double for your manager or boss and having frequent communications that are positive in nature is a vital component for any good employee-boss relationship. Having an open and positive communication channel with your corporate master will foster good relations and make them much happier with you as an employee/vassal all things being equal. Furthermore, having a happy boss at the office will make your life a whole lot easier, and more than pays for itself in the corporate long run. Therefore, make keeping your manager or boss happy the main priority at the office.

7 CORPORATIONS ARE ONE BIG GAME

In this chapter we discuss the social and behavioral dynamics of corporations. When you think about it, there is a lot of game playing going on in corporations. It starts with the interview process, the job candidate is marketing themselves in the best light possible with a bunch of half-truths, stretched accomplishments and outright lies.

The employer is putting together a job description which oftentimes is so broad that many candidates are completely wasting their time interviewing for the position because the employer and manager are just trying to broaden the applicant and talent pool. In many instances, human resources simply utilizes an outdated job description which has nothing to do with the actual job and the activities performed in the role.

During the interview process, the candidates spin the real reason they are looking for another job in the first place, and why things didn't work out at their previous companies.

Similarly the hiring manager doesn't advertise the fact that the real reason there are many job openings in this department is because they all hated working for this manager, and the work processes in this department or business unit are terrible. They will spin the narrative to say something like, "Well, we have some new projects that we received budgeting for, so we need to hire several new team members!"

The real truth is that several employees left as soon as they could find other jobs because the manager was a terrible micromanager, and the stress levels in the department were off the freaking charts.

You will find a lot of this going on in corporations, a whole lot of gameplaying and outright corporate fakeness. There are so many things that are fake in Corporate America, that you have to filter through the balderdash to get to the facts of the matter.

The companies will all talk about their great training programs, and when you actually start working at the company, your manager will not let you take the training classes you want, or doesn't want you wasting time taking training classes when you could be doing some additional project work. The typical manager response is, "Well, we have had recent budget cutbacks, so you cannot take those classes this year!"

Some more classic games that are played in Corporate America, is the literal treating of employees like babies, so much of mandated corporate training is complete balderdash. These are absolute waste of time courses, videos and presentations meant to condition employees for some office safety mandate, corporate corruption issue or company sponsored marketing materials.

These usually come through human resources and are complete time wasters typically devised to cover corporate's respective ass, and hopefully reduce liability issues for the company. Most of these company sponsored materials are discussing issues that are pretty much common sense to most employees who can fog up a mirror. These corporate materials are essentially designed as paternalistic, behavioral conditioning initiatives hoping to positively reinforce and condition employees like rats in a psychological experiment.

For instance, I cannot count the times that I was

subjected to anti-bribery act documentation materials to read and sign, as are most corporate employees. Meanwhile the executive team is often playing with a different set of rules than the rank and file employees at corporations. They are oftentimes all-in on winning large lucrative contracts regardless of the legal and regulatory costs and have been known to utilize corporate bribery slush funds to facilitate closing these big deals.

The corporate hypocrisy is palpable here, like really, you are sending the rank and file employees anti-bribery materials, whose job responsibilities will never even put them in a position to violate the anti-bribery act, and meanwhile the company has a high level strategy that relies heavily on violating this law.[12]

When working at a corporation you will see a lot of stupid stuff that equates to outright nannyism, and these corporate initiatives become complete time wasters for employees. The irony here is that these same corporations wonder why their employees cannot seem to get all their work done in an efficient and timely manner. For example, having an employee open a meeting with a safety moment, when the department and business unit in a corporate office doesn't do anything remotely dangerous besides reviewing spreadsheets, going to meetings, and talking on the phone is corporate nannyism at its finest.

This was BP's response for corporate office workers, all because the company's refining and offshore drilling operations were having safety compliance issues at an alarming rate.[13] BP would have been better served focusing all their safety training time, energy and resources where it

[12] https://www.justice.gov/opa/pr/hewlett-packard-russia-pleads-guilty-and-sentenced-bribery-russian-government-officials; https://www.investopedia.com/financial-edge/0512/the-biggest-bribe-cases-in-business-history.aspx
[13] https://en.wikipedia.org/wiki/Texas_City_Refinery_explosion; https://en.wikipedia.org/wiki/Deepwater_Horizon_explosion

actually matters, like out in the field where the safety issues were continually causing problems for the company. However, these types of corporate nannyism and overly paternalistic responses are so typical of Fortune 500 companies today.

These classic safety moments where employees are reminded to watch where they put that box at the office, and to avoid wearing headphones when they are running outdoors, in a meeting scheduled to discuss budgeting and cost overruns aptly illustrates the silliness of corporations these days. Moreover, the typical corporate response to any kind of incident where the company experiences a huge financial loss will be to go completely overboard with the corporate nannyism.

The corporation will instruct employees to make sure they hold onto the handrail when they are going down the stairs to properly condition and instill a safety mindset with employees at all times. Meanwhile, the indiscriminate cost-cutting measures and corporate shortcuts are creating the real dangerous liabilities and safety issues for the corporation. There is just so much corporate idiocy and absolute nonsense that happens all the time in corporations, and everyone just sort of plays along with the fakeness of it all.

As a matter of fact, pretty much everything about corporations requires a level of fakeness to it all, from meeting with clients and making sure they are happy with the exorbitant fees, hidden charges, and account padding that your company bills each month. Alternatively, to being on the other end of the business transaction, and meeting with suppliers who you are being fake with in accepting their gifts in the form of corporate account suite tickets to sporting events.

There is literally no end to corporate fakeness, suppliers will take you to dinner to ensure that you are happy with their services. A really good steak always makes you feel better about the supplier. The goal is to keep the account gatekeeper happy at all costs, so the supplier can keep charging your company an above market rate for their products and services.

There is so much unrestrained and unfettered bribery going on in American business dealings that corporate ethics is a complete oxymoron today. Who do you think buys all those corporate suites, and what do you think is the real purpose of those suites? It sure isn't to watch sporting and entertainment events. This is just a small portion of the dodgy corporate dealings that regularly occur in the business world, as most of the corporate monkey business takes place behind the scenes.

When you get on the inside of business dealings with regard to opaque contracts, murky side deals, and labyrinthine tax schemes, there are a lot of shenanigans that occur where you have to take a shower just to wash off the stench associated with the business proceedings.

It shouldn't surprise anyone that corporations are full of fakeness where everyone is just playing out the scripted game for appearances' sake, as corporations are just a microcosm of government these days with size ultimately determining the breadth and degree of power for the entity. And as we are all awfully familiar with in America, big government is the master of fakeness, playing the political game, and doings things for appearances' sake.

This is just par for the course in the purposeful game playing that performs a critical role in human societies, organizational culture, and human behavior. So play the fake games well, because you are going to see a lot of them in Corporate America. For example, the executive management team will have townhall meetings with the rank and file employees, and one of their primary talking points is usually diversity, and the importance of promoting diverse candidates into leadership positions.

What they really mean here is that they are all for

diversity so long as it doesn't affect their positions at the top of the corporate food chain, and that diversity is a good initiative for everyone else in the company to support in theory.

This is largely for show to the rank and file employees, as these people don't give a rat's ass about who gets promoted within the corporation. Just so long as it doesn't negatively affect their personal job security at the company. Most of these leadership types are full of balderdash. These people's biggest concern is when they can legally sell their company sponsored stock options, and how many times they can fly on the corporate jet.

This is another good one, "I don't believe in economic layoffs!" You might hear that corporate malarkey at a company sponsored townhall meeting. Meanwhile, management has sent a memo to human resources to scour departments and business units for places to cut costs in terms of employees, contractors, and business functions.

How about starting with the big-ticket items regarding salaried positions with the executives that don't really do anything at work. When you see what many of these executives actually do on a daily basis at corporations, you soon realize how much corporate excess there is at American companies. However, financial conditions will have to get really bad from an earnings standpoint before they start cutting their executive buddies' hefty salaries from the corporate payroll largesse.

It is best to take everything a corporate executive and upper management person says with a huge grain of salt. They didn't get to this position without being a major game player, and most things that come out of these people's mouths are fake corporate bromides and insipid gobbledygook speak. When you sit down and have dinner with these executives, you suddenly realize that they are not very bright, often completely full of balderdash, and many of these people are straight up hustlers.

These executives often don't have an ounce of talent besides being total corporate sycophants who were in the right place at the right time and play the game of corporate fakeness really well. Some people are just naturally good at being fake, and this all comes very easily for them. Oftentimes, these people are tall and relatively good-looking, and they speak good corporate nonsensical phrases that say virtually nothing of substance. These types of executives are dumb as rocks when you start peeling the layers with an in-depth conversation.

These corporate executives will start doing a lot of fake nodding in conversations, as they are masters of the universe with regard to the fake nod! These individuals hope like hell they can get through important dinner conversations and high-profile business lunches without being exposed for the enormously fake, talentless idiots that they truly are inside. Unfortunately, excellent game playing, an amiable personality and good personal style can go a long way in Corporate America, whitewashing a great amount of sheer incompetence and considerable ineptitude along the way.

Another point to be made about the fakeness you are going to find in Corporate America, is that the truth is its kryptonite. As a result, don't be a truth-seeker in corporations. This is because Corporate America doesn't actually want or value truth-seekers, and there is genuinely little room for truth-seekers in companies. There is just too damn much corporate fakeness and outright bad practices waiting to be exposed at the workplace. This means it is highly problematic to have a bunch of truth-seekers running around corporations these days.

Therefore, don't be a truth-seeker at your company, as this will only bring you lots of trouble, plenty of frustration and an army of enemies. The smart move here is learning how to play the game, or you won't last especially long in Corporate America. You just have to leap into the breach and play the corporate fakeness game in all its scintillating and specious glory.

This is why really smart people often have a hard time working in Corporate America. They are often natural born seekers of truth. The people who are smart and highly educated have been taught to learn the facts, acquire knowledge, examine what's behind the magician's sleight of hand, and search out the truth. It is rather apparent that these truth-seekers make a lot of enemies in a noticeably short period of time at corporations. This happens when they inevitably expose the truth, and routinely point out the massive incompetence, total mismanagement, and exceptionally bad practices of other employees.

These truth-seekers are upsetting the incompetent status quo that has been going on for years at the company, and quickly become huge targets to be destroyed by the other employees who are aggressively protecting their livelihood. In fact, truth-seekers are at odds with how the corporate game is played, and they must be defeated rather quickly, put in their place, or eliminated altogether.

There are entirely too many corrupt practices, inefficient and incompetent operations, and wide-ranging mismanagement waiting to be exposed by the truth-seekers in corporations these days. Thus, play the game according to the rules that have been in place for a long time in Corporate America, and avoid being obsessed with exposing the truth at your company as you will likely make life very difficult for yourself and your career.

Almost every conversation you have with colleagues at the office involves some level of fakeness. Hence as a new employee, you will need to learn the art of having fake conversations. They are actually very important for all employees to master, as you want to limit any real information that can be used against you by your fellow co-workers. This happens frequently in gossiping and character assassination conversations that inexorably circulate around the office.

Some people have very little work to do, seem to have endless time on their hands, and will make the corporate rounds spreading all kinds of gossip regarding other employees. Consequently, always be on guard concerning workplace conversations, and don't reveal anything personal about your life or work that can be used against you by your business colleagues.

People in general are far too revealing about their personal lives, and this is often used against them at some later day when relationships turn sour in life. Remember, that most things and certainly business relationships in corporations are built upon fakeness and insincerity, and these people are not truly your friends outside of the office environment.

Don't be gullible in this fake corporate environment and start revealing information about yourself that can be used against you in some negative fashion. It is amazing how the most innocent thing you divulge about yourself to the manager can be used against you when they have an axe to grind.

Do not try to be overly honest and reveal any of your weaknesses with regard to specific job skillsets or divulge any limitations in various areas regarding competency levels on a given project. The rationale here is that this information will likely be used against you at an inopportune time when the manager needs to justify some action that they take against you in some entirely unrelated matter.

I am not a fan with regard to many of Donald Trump's policies, but he has accurately recognized that in the cutthroat world of politics, that any weakness you reveal to your competitors will be used against you. It is wise to think in these terms while working in the corporation. Don't reveal any of your weaknesses to the colleagues at the office (whether we are talking about a physical or virtual office) because there is a high likelihood that it comes back to bite you in the end.

Just learn the fake niceties of the corporate conversation where you talk impartially about the weather, the economy, the local sports teams and maybe the state of your golf game for a more personal touch. However, if you can, try to steer the conversation towards letting business colleagues talk about themselves, as oftentimes people really like to talk about themselves in the corporate world. The end result is that you build effective communication channels and comfortable relationships with colleagues.

These are extremely important and very useful emotional and social intelligence tools that are necessary to work effectively with your business colleagues in the corporation.[14] Moreover, you accomplish this wonderful communication feat without revealing anything highly personal about yourself that is going to be viewed in a negative fashion or used adversely against you in some way down the road.

It would also be a suboptimal strategy to just hide in the proverbial corner, being the quiet little mouse working dutifully in their corporate cubicle, and not being very sociable or building valuable relationships. This strategy makes it rather difficult to advance past the working group level in climbing the corporate ladder. So learn how to have fake corporate conversations like everyone else at the office. It is important to master *the art of fakeness* without coming across as fake. It is quite a skill, as you can imagine. The really good ones have mastered this trick in the corporate world.

Just realize that most things in Corporate America are built on Fakeness, and part of playing the corporate game, and it is one giant game, is to master the art of being fake.

---

[14] https://en.wikipedia.org/wiki/Emotional_intelligence; https://en.wikipedia.org/wiki/Social_intelligence

You can fight this naturally occurring phenomenon in Corporate America, as I am sure there is some engineer right now in the corner doing this very thing with all their truth-seeking might. However, these people will always be stuck in the metaphorically speaking engineering roles, and routinely punished for their truth-seeking mentality at the company by colleagues and the Corporation as a whole. This is just a losing battle to fight in the long run.

In the end you make the personal choice. Are you trying to make life difficult for yourself, putting your head doggedly in the sand, or do you want to learn the rules of the game, and play the game of corporate politics to win versus your competitors? The choice is yours ultimately as you will be the one living with the consequences of your actions.

8 INTRODUCTION TO GAME THEORY

In this chapter we discuss Game Theory, which can be defined a number of ways, so we will start with some basic definitions. For example, there is the following definition: "Game theory is a theoretical framework for conceiving social situations among competing players. In some respects, game theory is the science of strategy, or at least the optimal decision-making of independent and competing actors in a strategic setting."[15]

Another definition of Game Theory: "The branch of mathematics concerned with the analysis of strategies for dealing with competitive situations where the outcome of a participant's choice of action depends critically on the actions of other participants. Game theory has been applied to contexts in war, business, and biology."[16]

And finally Wikipedia says, "Game theory is the study of mathematical models of strategic interaction among rational decision-makers. It has applications in all fields of social science, as well as in logic, systems science and computer science. Originally, it addressed zero-sum games, in which each participant's gains or losses are exactly balanced by those of the other participants. Today, game theory applies to a wide range of behavioral relations, and

---

[15] https://www.investopedia.com/terms/g/gametheory.asp
[16] https://www.lexico.com/definition/game_theory

is now an umbrella term for the science of logical decision making in humans, animals, and computers."[17]

So now that we have covered the formal definitions of Game Theory from an academic standpoint, let me break the principles of Game Theory down for our purposes here in the corporate world. The world of large corporations is one where agents are routinely making strategic decisions against a background of known and unknown variables. Furthermore, there are decidedly different outcomes with profound costs associated with these decisions at play here for corporate professionals.

We aren't going to draw out a prisoner's dilemma payoff matrix for decisions that employees typically face in the corporate setting. Sure we could build a model and assign mathematical values to the different choices in specific problem scenarios, but this isn't how an agent would typically act in the real world of Corporate America. These corporate decisions are often made on the fly, and the agent needs to utilize rough heuristics or conceptual shortcuts to make quick decisions in the midst of a chaotic and often unscripted workplace environment.

The agent needs to think about the big picture concepts regarding Game Theory and the rationale behind different courses of action. Moreover, the agent must be able to apply these Game Theory principles to ever-changing and differing scenarios that consistently present themselves in the corporate environment.

In the corporate world, professionals are constantly challenged with new problems that arise from this social setting, and they need to have the mental software and reasoning skillset to solve these problems over the course of their careers. This is especially important if they hope to

---

[17] https://en.wikipedia.org/wiki/Game_theory; Myerson, Roger B. (1991). Game Theory: Analysis of Conflict, Harvard University Press, p. 1.

advance towards much higher levels within the organization.

This is what some of the most skilled game players do in real world situations where they have to make relatively quick decisions in games like chess, poker, blackjack, sports betting, and a multitude of other strategy-based games.

For example, a good poker player understands the basic math behind the decisions, but they are simultaneously computing several other game theory concepts regarding each decision, like "What information does my opponent have regarding my tendencies," and "My opponent knows that I go all-in with these types of hand ranges when I am short stacked," and "What kind of story am I telling with a bluff in this spot?"

The game of poker is a great game with a lot of similarities to the corporate world because many agents are trying to deceive each other as to their true intentions to gain an advantage in playing the game. The experienced poker player has been in similar situations where they have created an internal database in their head regarding several different strategies that can be applied to each specific scenario they will face in a game of poker. These players quickly run through the available strategy options, and choose the best option considering their opponents and the likely actions to their given strategy decision.

The game theory work has been done beforehand, as they have run the calculations and scenarios over a million times in their head. By the time they are experienced professional poker players, the real-time decisions have become very simple and easy to execute for these game players. These important decisions with monetary implications on the line become automatic decision tree algorithms for these skilled players at the poker table.

This is where you want to get to from a Corporate Game Theory standpoint, where you have thought about all the specific options, calculated all the likely outcomes of each decision, and stored these scenarios in your brain for future reference. Thus, when the situation arises, you have already worked out the optimal move. As a result, you always make the correct play or proper decision in the real-time scenario that presents itself in the workplace environment.

Consequently, you need to do the work beforehand, go over the common scenarios, and write down all the available options that you have to solve a given problem or conflict scenario at the office. You need to think deeply about these corporate scenarios, from a meta-standpoint, or from a bird's eye view of the problem that you are evaluating. This will help you come up with likely outcomes for each option both from your perspective and from the other agents involved in the problem. You need to think hard about the other agents involved in the corporate scenario and their likely responses.

The next course of action is to rank the options on a scale from 1 to 5, with 1 being the best rating, and 5 being the worst rated option. You can also draw out an actual decision tree for each option involved in the overall problem. This will enable you to think deeply about the problem and train your mind to think logically and rationally in strategizing about the various options available to you as a game player.

Decision trees are really simple to master and easy to learn. Just go online and look at examples of common decision tree models and start practicing with everyday problem scenarios that you have with friends and family members. For instance, utilize decision trees to try and solve difficult financial problems or resolve complicated disagreements with friends and family members that create stress for you outside of the office.

Once you start getting better at thinking strategically and analyzing everyday life and family problems from a bird's eye view perspective, then you can start applying these problem analysis tools towards scenarios you have faced in the past at the corporate office. This will be good preparation for the new challenges you will surely face in the future with corporate colleagues.

In reality, human beings are very bad at this kind of thinking. This is why neighborhood disputes often escalate wildly out of control from rather small beginnings. A homeowner's dog is off the leash and frightens their neighbor's kid, so they call the police. This initial neighborhood incident causes another round of actions and reactions on behalf of both neighbors, and next thing you know things have escalated to the point of verbal threats and physical assaults.

When you go over a given move available to you at the corporation, you need to think thoroughly about how the other party will likely react to your move, and are there some unintended consequences regarding this move that you might not like in the end? These strategies, options and decisions don't operate in a vacuum! There are moves, reactions to moves, counter moves, and even unintended consequences that you need to consider when evaluating Corporate Game Problems.

Just like in football when the defense blitzes the offense in trying to pressure the quarterback. Well this means that there are less defenders downfield covering offensive players, and if the blitz doesn't get to the quarterback in time, the defense risks being susceptible to a big play by the offense. Therefore, a lot of strategy, calculations and game theory goes into evaluating whether it is a good idea to blitz at a given point in the game.

The same goes for evaluating whether you should confront your boss over an instance where you feel they are being unfair, and what the likely response would be by your boss versus the other option of just letting it slide. Moreover, what are the ramifications of this choice versus other courses of action like seeking advice from a mentor, going to human resources, or escalating the issue above your direct chain of command.

For instance, if you are a mid-level manager and are thinking about putting an employee under you on PIP, you need to really think through what you are trying to achieve in this situation. Are you trying to get rid of the employee? Do you want to keep this employee? How much corporate time and resources have gone into training this employee? If you truly want to keep the employee, and you want to help the employee improve their performance, ask yourself if putting them on PIP is the best way to accomplish this goal.

Is this employee really underperforming their work responsibilities or am I putting them on PIP for other personal reasons such as I don't really like their personality? What is the likely response from the employee who is being put on PIP? Will the employee be blindsided by this PIP course of action? Is there an intermediary step that you should take as a manager to inform the employee that you are concerned about their job performance, and if you don't see noticeable improvement in their performance by a specific date, then being put on PIP is the next step towards addressing this underperformance with the employee.

These are the types of questions and scenarios that you need to play out in your mind as a manager before taking a given course of action. Unfortunately, I have seen managers not really think things through and implement all kinds of horrible policies, terrible practices, and poorly planned project scopes at major corporations. These corporate managers routinely fail to sufficiently evaluate the entire problem, think through their potential options, and properly account for any unintended consequences that may arise.

This is setting yourself up for a lot of future stress as a manager if you are regularly making these types of shortsighted personnel decisions without fully evaluating these problems and scenarios from all the different angles. This is a poor way to play the game, you are setting yourself up for failure as a manager and making a lot of enemies along the way.

You need to map out these angles and options on paper until you get really good at doing these game theory calculations in your head. You need to think, understand, and know what the likely actions, reactions, countermoves, and unintended consequences are for each branch on your decision tree. As a manager or employee you need to get in the habit of modeling the problems you are facing at work with well-thought-out decision trees. These decision trees will really help you understand the overall problem dynamics much better, and provide a solid basis for making rational, well-informed decisions in the corporate world.

Sometimes these are not easy options, as two options may be highly dependent upon unpredictable variables, ever-changing factors, and unknowable information. However, if you really think about the problem in this much detail, enough to write down option branches on a decision tree model, then you will be making decisions on the basis of a full and comprehensive understanding of the problem.

It is just as important to understand what you don't know about the problem dynamics, as well as the things that you do know with absolute certainty. If these were easy issues to deal with, then they wouldn't be problems in the first place. This is half the battle in problem solving; properly identifying and outlining the unpredictable variables, ever-changing factors, and unknowable information of the problem dynamics.

What you don't want to occur is making impulsive, emotionally based decisions when you haven't examined the problem in great detail. As a corporate game player you are at a major disadvantage when you fail to think through all your available options when resolving problems.

This is especially true with regard to problems arising from corporate and office politics. In this case, you are making a decision from a position of weakness and an overall lack of quality information, which equates to an uninformed choice in the end. This is tantamount to abandoning logical reasoning and strategic planning altogether in trying to solve these complex corporate problems. This is definitely not the best way to go about playing the corporate game.

You might make the right move, but since you haven't fully evaluated your options, and the unintended consequences associated with those various options, then this would be through sheer luck. You might as well carry a rabbit's foot around with you at the office and start consulting fortune tellers regarding your work-related problems. This is a dreadfully bad and irrational way to approach the decision-making process in resolving challenging problems. In other words, it fails to take advantage of game theory principles in making smarter decisions which inevitably leads to better outcomes in the corporate world.

You are trying to make smart, well-informed, strategically valid decisions at the corporation. The goal is to avoid recklessly gambling with your important career. Afterall, this isn't why you spent all that time and money studying in college for a corporate career.

You didn't jump through all those ridiculous administrative hoops in college because you thoroughly enjoy accumulating massive student loan debt. You didn't dedicate yourself to obtaining noteworthy professional certifications because you have so much free time on your hands.

You achieved these important developmental milestones to land a valuable opportunity to advance your career at a Fortune 500 company. You sure didn't put in all this hard work to just carelessly throw it all away on a series of impulsive and uninformed decisions that are cleverly disguised as gambling exercises with extremely poor odds. This is just too damn important not to include cutting edge game theory principles and strategic thinking into your overall decision-making process at the corporation.

9 IT'S ALL GAME THEORY

In this chapter we discuss the similarities between playing games like chess and poker and navigating the corporate environment. You may not enjoy playing games in general or playing games such as chess and poker, but now would be a good time to take the leap and start playing these types of strategy games. In fact, learning to play both of these games will give you an entirely new perspective on game playing in the corporate world.

The games of chess and poker both rely heavily on strategy, but there are psychological elements involved in these games as well. If you are relatively new to these games, many of you will be surprised just how comparable the game playing skillsets are between these strategy games and the corporate environment.

I would recommend getting your feet wet by creating an account on Chess.com.[18] This is a great website for learning and playing the game of chess. It has a lot of great ideas, people and resources designed for creating a friendly environment around the game of chess which is both educational with regard to game theory and enjoyable at the same time.

The basic membership is free, and it is a good place to

---

[18] https://www.chess.com/

start thinking conceptually about moves that you make on a chessboard and studying the opponent's reactions to your moves. This will help you learn to think several moves ahead, and ultimately discover the art of setting traps. You will begin recognizing traps set by your opponents and develop a good understanding regarding the pros and cons of different chess strategies.

In playing chess you also have to learn how to handle your emotions from a psychological standpoint. The game of chess teaches you a lot about yourself from a mental standpoint. It reveals your psychological strengths and weaknesses as a game player. It is important how you react to mistakes, obnoxious players, a series of disappointing games, and being made to look foolish by better and more experienced players in the game. You soon realize that underestimating opponents will cost you dearly, and that if you don't *Bring Your A-Game*, you can really play well below your talent and skill level.

One can start to appreciate how this game theory knowledge is applicable and transferable to the corporate world. If you don't bring your A-Game at the office on a project you are going to look bad in front of colleagues, managers, and external stakeholders. We all have different gears that we can go to regarding performance levels, and sometimes it is natural to coast in the cushy world of corporate annual salaries and great perquisites. However, coasting at the wrong time in corporations can be deadly, especially if your manager or their boss notices your C-Game on a project.

In this case, you have just given the people that control your future in terms of bonuses and promotions at the company a bad impression regarding your abilities which may be hard to overcome. As once people in general and managers specifically make evaluations about others, these initial conclusions almost seem set in stone for many people. This always becomes their fallback opinion of your abilities and performance, even if you start performing entirely better in your role at the company. This is why it is so important to bring your A-Game to the office as much as possible, as your Corporate Overlords will use your C-Game against you come performance review time.

If nothing else, the game of Chess will work your brain, keeping your mind mentally sharp and paying attention to the smaller details at work and in life. It is similar to playing brain games to keep your mind sharp, mentally alert, and focused. So play a game before work or solve some chess puzzles with your morning coffee. This will get your brain working before the stress of the corporate environment where you will meet the real game players.

The game of live poker is a genuinely good game to play to get you thinking about game theory implications involved with the different options available to you when making strategic moves. The game of live poker is certainly a game about psychology, human behavior, social interactions, and overall situational awareness in a highly competitive environment.

In comparison, the bigger picture view of the corporate world is also one characterized by a highly competitive environment where everyone is playing the game in a self-interested manner for essentially a limited supply of corporate real estate, hierarchical legitimacy, and overall power. The endgame being to flourish and rise up the corporate ladder while stepping over the competition along the way.

The money in poker provides the stakes which adds pressure to the game in general, and specifically in making good decisions under pressure packed situations at the table. The money dynamic makes the game more compelling and interesting to players but also brings its own set of frustrations and problems. This is for the reason that deep down inside human psyches, in a viscerally palpable and instinctual manner, people really hate losing money.

Human beings in general will do some absolute insane things over money matters, and a game like poker with money playing such a central role in defining winners and losers will really test human emotions. In fact, people will start fights with other players and do some crazy things in the game of poker when they lose control of their emotions.

These individuals have basically lost their minds over a game of cards and have been unable to keep their cool under the pressure packed scenarios that inevitably present themselves and make the game interesting in the first place. Consequently, the game of poker brings out some of the worst qualities and behaviors in human beings.

There are people who are remarkably successful in managing emotions in their personal and professional lives but will often have a hard time keeping their emotions in check at the poker table. This is often an ego-driven behavior as these people are just not used to losing much in life and are outside of their normal comfort zone.

Playing live poker is a good way to study human behavior in a stressful game playing environment. If you can learn to keep your cool and not get drawn into mistakes by your opponents who are often behaving badly, being overly aggressive, acting irrationally and playing poorly at the poker table, this will put you in good stead at the office.

It is just a certainty in your corporate career that some colleague, manager, or important client will say something that is terribly negative, clearly derogatory, highly argumentative, openly hostile, and just plain mean-spirited in the course of your business interactions.

There is oftentimes some underlying problem or deeper conflict responsible for these contentious corporate interactions and regrettable behaviors at the office. Sometimes you are in tough negotiations with outside firms and are fighting over financial terms. In other situations you are competing with business colleagues for an important account, coveted promotion, or high-profile project at the company. Whatever the case may be, you can expect to have difficult interactions and unfriendly conversations with business colleagues in the corporate world.

This is an important point that I am going to make here so pay close attention. You often cannot control what other people do in this world, whether at the poker table or at the office, but you can definitely control how you react to what they do. It is not the event that really matters, it is how you react to the event that is more important. In regard to the big picture of playing the Corporate Game, it is important to react well to turbulent events at the office. And trust me, there will be plenty of turbulent events and rough seas to navigate well during your corporate career.

In poker, going on tilt is defined as the following:

> Tilt originated as a poker term for a state of mental or emotional confusion or frustration in which a player adopts a less than optimal strategy, usually resulting in the player becoming over-aggressive. Tilting is closely associated with another poker term, "steam". Placing an opponent on tilt or dealing with being on tilt oneself is an important aspect of poker. It is a relatively frequent occurrence due to frustration, animosity against other players, or simply bad luck.[19]

This idea of tilt is applicable to the world of Corporate America, it really is all Game Theory in the end, as you are always worse off in playing any game when you go on tilt period. It is not the "bad beat" at the poker table that kills you, it is how you react to the really unlucky set of

---

[19] https://en.wikipedia.org/wiki/Tilt_(poker);
https://www.cardschat.com/tilt.php

circumstances that hurts you the most. This is the same at the office, when your boss gives you a "bad beat" by giving the important account or project to a competitor, it is how you react to this unfortunate set of circumstances that makes a big difference during the course of your career.

Do you bitterly sulk and mope around the office when things don't go your way? Do you make bad situations and negative outcomes worse by performing poorly in your role and having a terrible attitude? Alternatively, do you congratulate your business colleagues, and offer to help them in any way possible when they are the victors? Do you have a positive attitude despite losing out on promotions, business opportunities and important projects?

It is definitely advantageous to maintain and project a positive attitude and enthusiastically friendly persona at all times and under any circumstances in the corporate world. Furthermore, we are talking about the good, the bad and the everything in between with regard to the aforementioned *any circumstances* reference.

This is playing the game optimally, and your manager, business colleagues and upper management will respect you more as a competitor and valued team member when you can handle losing gracefully at the office. This winning attitude will go a long way in helping you play the game better than most of your fellow competitors in the corporate world.

This should also motivate you to play the Corporate Game with a little more vigor and dedicated work ethic. These corporate losses should serve to refocus your efforts on working a bit harder and being a little more determined not to let these workplace defeats happen again.

You often get motivated in life and learn more from your battle defeats and individual failures than you do from your victories and successes. The same reasoning applies to losing battles and taking losses in the corporate world. Moreover, just because you lose a set in a game of tennis doesn't mean you have lost the match. There is always the next match to be played over the following years in your company when you are going to be much better at playing the Corporate Game.

I will repeat this concept because it is that important, and you need to carry this thought with you throughout your corporate career and the interactions that you have with the various game playing opponents. It isn't the event; it is how you react to the event. You definitely have a choice in this matter. You are not living in a totally deterministic world with no ability to control your emotions, behaviors and reactions to events that take place in life and the corporate world.

There is a lot of Game Theory that goes into how you play your poker hands, betting strategies, and how often you should bluff in the game. There is considerable research and thought regarding playing a short stack of chips at the table, and how to play against aggressive and passive players. There is also strategic thinking concerning which hands you should play in certain positions from the button, and how to put your opponents on various hand ranges. The list is endless on the subject of Game Theory as it applies to the competition of live poker. This is what makes it such an excellent game to learn, and an even more interesting game to play.

The readers will have to trust me on the similarities between the game of live poker and the corporate world. When you start playing live poker you will understand a lot of the parallels to those interactions with people in the corporate world. For instance, common poker thoughts like "What can you actually beat here, really only a bluff!" and "Am I truly getting good pot odds to make this call?"

This kind of Game Theory thinking applies to the same decision-making process that regularly occurs in the corporate world as well. For example, typical corporate thoughts such as "What do I realistically have to gain by escalating this problem I have with my manager?" and "What is the risk/reward associated with making this deal?" and finally "Do I really want to burn my objection capital at the corporation with this particular issue?"

In this day and age, most cities have cardrooms where you can play live poker as poker clubs have opened up as alternatives in getting around prohibitive state laws. There are also plenty of casinos which are within driving distance to most major cities in America. In addition, there are casinos on Indian reservations and reputable underground games that are safe and friendly places to experience the game of poker. And finally, there are many home games that can be found in your local area via online resources. A good poker resource is TwoPlusTwo.com where you can find local games, learn about poker strategies, and study high-level game theory.[20] In the end, the game of live poker is really a game about people.

Once you find a regular game, start studying some basic poker game theory and incorporating these concepts into your decision-making process at the table. A good longer-term goal is to keep exercising your mind with challenging game theory scenarios, getting better at analyzing your opponents, and trying to eventually become a winning player at the local $1/$3 No-Limit Hold'em cash game. However, don't worry about the daily poker results because you may have a couple of professional poker players who are sharks at your table.

Always keep the broader perspective in mind, you are playing live poker to develop a good understanding of Game Theory principles in action and make better decisions at the table. The ultimate goal is not to become a professional poker player, but to transfer this improved decision-making skillset which is backed by solid game theory analysis and principles to those difficult decisions

[20] https://www.twoplustwo.com/

you routinely encounter in the corporate world.

The game of live poker has its own unique dynamics. For instance, those professional poker sharks are the experts in the local game, and the rest of the players are rank amateurs, recreational players, and solid regulars. The great thing about the game of poker is that good recreational players can often hold their own with professional players over the short term. In most other sports and games this just isn't possible. However, over the long term, the professional players will have a significant winrate advantage over the good recreational players.[21]

In point of fact, professional poker players have to use some Game Theory strategy in keeping the fish happy. For instance, most of the recreational and casual poker players who do something else for a living are referred to as the fish. The professionals are the sharks, and the rest of the players in the player pool are similar to the fish in the ocean. However, the sharks use a little bit of strategy referred to as *"Don't Tap the Glass!"* This phrase comes from not tapping the glass at the aquarium and scaring the fish away.

Well, the good poker professionals like Chip Reese and Doyle Brunson developed an entire relationship strategy and behavioral style around keeping the fish and big whales happy in the games they regularly played.[22] The goal is not to ridicule these players for inferior play or winning in a gloating and superior behavioral manner. The idea is that you don't want to run off your good customers. And in this case, the good customers are the ones providing consistent revenue for the established poker professionals.

Hence, learning how to be a good winner is important in

---

[21] https://www.888poker.com/magazine/strategy/poker-winrate; http://www.thepokerbank.com/strategy/other/winrate/
[22] https://en.wikipedia.org/wiki/Chip_Reese; https://en.wikipedia.org/wiki/Doyle_Brunson

life, as well as the poker table and in the corporate world. It is a good idea to avoid rubbing the fact that you are winning the game into your opponents' faces. It is much better to play the long game and be a gracious winner.

The good poker professionals know how to select the best games with wealthy individuals who play poker as a recreational hobby. These individuals can afford to lose discretionary income on a regular basis. The experienced poker professionals have learned how to act and behave in such an amicable manner that their opponents keep coming back for more. This occurs despite losing money consistently in these games.

It is quite a skill when you think about it on the whole, as the opponents realize they are sizable underdogs in these games, yet they continue to be agreeable to the terms of this predatory relationship. The predatory relationship has clearly defined outcomes for the recreational players, as they consistently lose money to the good professional players.

In other words, the game environment provides enough happiness and overall enjoyment that the financial considerations of this relationship are secondary in nature. However, the poker professionals have to be smart about this poker tactic and game selection strategy, as it doesn't take much to make people unhappy with this type of arrangement. On the grounds that it is undeniably a predatory relationship in the end.

In this game environment many whales enjoy having their egos stroked by the poker professionals. The game discussions often revolve around how talented these individuals are in their chosen professions. The wealthy players with a business background are praised for their great business acumen and personal achievements. The professional poker players laud these wealthy individuals for being extremely knowledgeable about life and lionizing their celebrity status when appropriate.

The professional players talk about being extremely fortunate in soaking up all this incredible wisdom from these important and wealthy individuals. The operative term here being *wealthy* in this game playing environment. This rhetorical splendor wafts through the poker air while the professional players take the wealthy individuals' money. This is how the game is played at the elite level of high-stakes poker, which is actually a game within the game. This can all be summed up as not tapping the glass and keeping a nice playing environment for the fish and whales in the overall poker ecosystem.

Interestingly enough, this paradise for poker sharks can be ruined by some knucklehead player that comes along and starts demeaning the fish or whales for playing very poorly at the table. This shortsighted player spoils the party for the professional sharks who worked so hard creating this ideal money-making environment in the first place.

The professional sharks try to keep these poker loose cannons in line as there are serious business interests at stake in these games. After all, these good professional players make their considerable livelihoods by creating the right ambiance for others to have fun losing money to them.

It so happens that some whales are pretty sophisticated and realize they are being manipulated by the professional poker players. In this case, the incessant kissing up and ego stroking is actually a bad strategy and requires a more nuanced and sagacious approach. The professional players are usually rather good at reading people and their radar is highly tuned to the needs and requirements of the poker whales. The last thing experienced poker professionals want to do is offend their good paying customers.

However, it happens from time to time, and I have certainly witnessed whales being irritated at the poker table when they realize that the ego stroking is insincere flattery at best and downright condescending and demeaning at worse. The absolute worst-case scenario for professional poker players is having their best customers feel like they are being taken advantage of at the poker table.

These whales are often quite successful in their chosen profession outside of poker and being seen as essentially easy marks for grifting behavior is not going to make these people happy. This will definitely get in the way of enjoying the overall poker playing experience. But more importantly, the whales sure aren't going to sign up for this kind of public humiliation in the future. Remember, the goal is to keep these whales happy and coming back for more blissfully content losing poker sessions.

As a result, the good professional poker players adjust their whale handling strategy. Instead of the incessant kissing up and ego stroking approach, this is replaced with just straightforward respectful and well-mannered behavior. Oftentimes, the less is more approach gets the job done in life, especially with regard to more favorable communications and agreeable social interactions.

In summary, the really experienced professional poker players are remarkably subtle in this strategy of not tapping the glass. So much so that the poker fish and whales never really get the feeling they are being exploited and manipulated in this game within the game that exists in the poker ecosystem.

Well, the same goes for the office with regard to your manager and executive handling strategy. There are managers and executives who enjoy having others kissing up to them at work, putting them on pedestals and stroking their respective egos. However, these are often incompetent doltish managers and injudicious executives in the corporate world, so this kissing up strategy works rather well. On the other hand, really competent managers and perspicacious executives see right through this spurious behavior and do not like it in the slightest.

Indeed, accomplished managers and knowledgeable

executives may realize this is part of office culture, and a viable strategy that many corporate employees use on a regular basis, but that does not mean they genuinely like this phony behavior. As a matter of fact, these smart corporate managers and wise executives are making mental notes of this conspicuously fake behavior, and you are losing points and sacrificing overall respect in employing this false flattery approach at the office.

So just as a professional poker player needs to know what buttons to push in extracting the most money from the fish and whales at the poker table and keeping these good customers blissfully happy during this process. The same goes for the corporate world, you need to realize what strategies to implement with different people at the office.

For instance, if some managers and executives really are so insecure and misguided that it is advantageous for you to utilize the kissing up strategy, that this approach makes your life easier as an employee at the corporation, then play the game according to these rules defined by your specific situation and embrace this kissing up strategy. As this is the Optimal Game Theory strategy in this particular circumstance but pay attention when you notice managers and executives who truly dislike this practice.

It is vitally important to properly identify which corporate managers and executives actually resent this kissing up strategy and do not respect people who use this tactic at the office. In short, know your audience at all times in the corporate world.

There are innumerable similarities between behavioral strategy games like live poker and the corporate world. For instance, just like at the poker table you have to know your opponents thoroughly and have studied enough players to be able to spot various player types. This information is utilized in adapting your game playing strategies to the specific types of players that you are competing against in the game.

Well, the same goes for other employees, managers, business colleagues, big bosses, high-level executives, and outside clients that you encounter while working at the corporation. It is crucial to adjust the strategies according to your opponents, as certain game theory strategies are optimal in some circumstances, and suboptimal in other situations. You have to be a creative thinker in the corporate world, it is certainly disadvantageous to just go around making impulsive unthinking decisions at the office. This will get you in a lot of trouble throughout your corporate career.

In the end, *It's all Game Theory*, so think through the problems you encounter at the office like playing a hand in a poker game. For example, run through your playing scenarios and available options, think about your various game playing strategies, perform your cost benefit calculations, and then choose the course of action with the highest expected value for this particular situation.[23]

This isn't an exact science; sure you could make it more scientific with formal modeling methodology by utilizing precise values and numbers. Though this isn't that practical for most employees at the office, so just rank your options using a rough value system and calculate an extrapolated version of expected value for your decisions.

Normally, expected value calculations are considered over the long run or a large sample size of similar decisions. However, due to the fact that the office dynamic often has unique variables that are situation specific, and the costs are extremely high if you make the wrong decision in a given case. Therefore, the corporate environment requires placing more importance on this

---

[23] https://en.wikipedia.org/wiki/Expected_value;
https://www.investopedia.com/terms/e/expected-value.asp;
https://www.cardschat.com/poker-odds-expected-value.php;
https://en.wikibooks.org/wiki/Poker/Expected_value

specific set of circumstances versus the long run calculus of similar decisions.

There might not be a long run if you truly make the incorrect decision at the office and things spiral wildly out of control in your life. This is serious business here, as these are often life altering decisions that we make in the corporate world.

The fact that these decisions at the corporation often have life changing implications for people is actually a variable in itself that carries weight in the overall Game Theory calculus. Consequently, it is often wise to go with the conservative choice in a given situation.

As one must have a healthy respect for the very notion of Risk when making these complicated important decisions in the corporate world. The Risk Factor should never be underestimated in properly analyzing and competently solving these complex problems, challenging scenarios, and daunting dilemmas that regularly present themselves at the office.

As you can logically understand, the actively thinking game player who calculates Game Theory strategies has a definitive advantage over their coworkers who consistently make impulsive and unthinking decisions in addressing their problems at the office. These injudicious decisions often have unintended consequences and negative outcomes that corporate employees never really consider in their decision-making process.

It is only after the damage has already been done that these corporate employees have severe regrets about how they handled these problems and situations from a methodology standpoint. These individuals wish they would have methodically worked through their problems and thought extensively about the available options before acting on their respective issues in such an impulsive and often emotionally charged manner. In short, failing to think before you react is rarely a good strategy in Corporate

America.

One of the reasons why I decided to write this book is because so many corporate employees don't think things through very well at the office. They routinely make a bunch of emotionally charged and impulsive decisions that are suboptimal from a Game Theory standpoint, and truly hinder their corporate careers in the process.

10 SUN TZU

In this chapter we will discuss some theory regarding business and workplace strategy. I first became familiar with Sun Tzu through the medium of movies in my youth. Sun Tzu was a Chinese general in the late sixth century BCE who thought a lot about military strategy and made keen observations about human behavior in the course of military battles. The knowledge acquired from leading soldiers into war and the experience of these battles inspired Sun Tzu to write a military strategy treatise known as The Art of War.[24]

I was first introduced to Sun Tzu while watching the movie Wall Street which was directed by Oliver Stone, and co-written by Oliver Stone and Stanley Weiser.[25] This is a very good movie, and definitely in the upper echelon of movies that explore the fascinating world of high finance, business dealmaking and financial markets.

In the movie there are several scenes where Sun Tzu strategy is used to make points about the world of business on Wall Street. For example, in one scene Bud Fox says,

---

[24] https://en.wikipedia.org/wiki/Sun_Tzu;
http://classics.mit.edu/Tzu/artwar.html;
https://www.history.com/topics/ancient-china/the-art-of-war
[25] https://en.wikipedia.org/wiki/Wall_Street_(1987_film);
http://www.moviediva.com/website/MD_root/reviewpages/MD_WallStreet.htm

"Sun-tzu: If your enemy is superior, evade him. If angry, irritate him. If equally matched, fight, and if not split and reevaluate."[26] And in another scene Gordon Gekko says, "I don't throw darts at a board. I bet on sure things. Read Sun-tzu, The Art of War. Every battle is won before it is ever fought."[27]

Sun Tzu military strategy and the teachings of Lao Tzu, who was a Chinese philosopher and the believed author of the Tao Te Ching, along with several other eastern based thinkers were heavily influential in Japanese business strategy and management principles.[28]

Japanese companies were really strong in the 1970s and 1980s, and American companies started studying some of their business strategies and influences.[29] As a result, Sun Tzu and other Japanese business influences started circulating around American Corporations in the 1980s especially.

The world of ideas represents a give and take model, and ultimately when someone has success people take notice. The industry leaders try to incorporate some of these best practices into their business or organizational thinking. Thus, in the late 1980s on Wall Street a bunch of financial players were throwing around Sun Tzu quotes like they were going out of style.

In more recent history, Tony Soprano in the HBO produced television series *The Sopranos*, discussed the idea that the strategic thinking articulated in The Art of War was

---

[26] http://www.artofwarsuntzu.com/suntzuandhollywood.htm
[27] https://www.marketwatch.com/story/happy-birthday-gordon-gekko-my-5-favorite-quotes-from-the-wall-street-villain-2019-05-06
[28] Chen, Min **Asian Management Systems**: *Chinese, Japanese and Korean Styles of Business.* March 2004. (p. 34).
https://prodygia.com/chinasimplified/articles/61-a-primer-on-chinese-philosophy-confucius-lao-tzu-taoism-sun-tzu-art-of-war
[29] http://factsanddetails.com/japan/cat24/sub155/item903.html;
https://en.wikipedia.org/wiki/Rising_Sun_(novel)

still relevant and particularly insightful with regard to the New Jersey mafia world.[30]

In my consulting world, I started to realize that there was a lot of military strategy and multi-level thinking taking place within the landscape of everyday Corporate America. I am not just referring to the world of corporate executives either, as in most Fortune 500 companies there are a lot of sophisticated, highly educated people walking around those corridors.

The reality of the situation reveals that there is definitely a lot of military precision subterfuge going on in the corporate world, and it became apparent to me that anybody trying to stay afloat in this turbulent and complex environment, better understand some of the strategic thinking and military strategy concepts conveyed by Sun Tzu in The Art of War.

You don't have to study all the Eastern Philosophers and memorize all of the Sun Tzu quotes, but it is a good idea to be familiar with some of the basic concepts underlying the thinking. Likewise, it is important to realize that there are real strategies to be considered at the office in making decisions and solving problems. Importantly, there is still a lot in common today with these historically relevant ideas, ancient teachings, and philosophical thinking.

Whether it is military strategy going all the way back to ancient China, Japan's dominance in business during the 1980s, or trying to resolve difficult issues today in Corporate America, the common thread is human beings and their range of behaviors.

Hence, it always confers an advantage to understand game theory principles, strategic thinking, and optimal play for evaluating a range of potential options in trying to solve challenging problems and make important decisions. This

---

[30] http://www.artofwarsuntzu.com/suntzuandhollywood.htm; https://en.wikipedia.org/wiki/The_Sopranos

is an important skillset in life, as well as the corporate world.

In summary, corporations are a brutal world these days with plenty of backstabbing, infighting, and creative sabotage, along with alliance building, networking, social positioning, and incessant subterfuge occurring on a regular basis. This happens on the ground floor of departmental cubicles, enclosed management offices, and countless conference rooms like an unabated plague with severe consequences for the uninitiated.

This social and political maneuvering is determining your fate as a corporate employee whether you realize it or not. You need to know all the available strategies to thrive and flourish in this game playing environment that mercilessly and relentlessly permeates the air and ethos of the modern corporation.

Let us review some Sun Tzu quotes from The Art of War.[31]

"Ponder and deliberate before you make a move."

Many times at the office you will be in discussions with colleagues, business managers and bosses, and they will say something stupid to you without deliberating or thinking about it beforehand. Oftentimes, this is a negative comment or an extremely poor choice of words. In some cases, the comments are just downright insulting and patently absurd.

The natural tendency is to snap back at this person, correct them on the spot, or show your sincere displeasure through nonverbal body language. However, this would be a miscalculation on your part, as you just witnessed this person make an obvious and unforgivable mistake in

---

[31] https://www.amazon.com/Art-War-Sun-Tzu/dp/1599869772; https://www.brainyquote.com/authors/sun-tzu-quotes

playing the corporate game. This professional colleague, business manager or corporate boss just crossed the line of acceptable behavior from a formal protocol standpoint.

If these corporate professionals actually thought about the situation strategically, they would use some euphemism, couch the negative in better terms, or avoid saying something absurd altogether. This is just how the game is played in the corporate world. You just don't say things that come into your head on an emotional impulse, that is playing the strategic game poorly, and routinely going to get corporate professionals in trouble at the office.

One compounds the problem by responding poorly to corporate professionals who have made communication mistakes or are behaving poorly at the office. This is falling into the trap of returning serve so to speak. Moreover, everyone always seems to place more importance on the reaction to the initial poor choice of words or inappropriate and unprofessional behavior in these conflict situations.

This is because the reaction or return of serve often has some real heat or strong emotions behind it. The usual way this plays out is that the initial offending statement or poor behavior is debated internally, and ultimately minimized in significance, but everyone agrees that the reaction or return of serve was definitely out of line.

These are the types of typical games that are played in Corporate America, and the best way to play this game is to simply make a mental note of the comment and continue on with productive work. Make no mistake, coworkers will take mental notes of these communication mistakes as well. Nevertheless, absolutely do not react on the spot in any manner.

It doesn't matter what is being said, how negative it is, or the level of absurdity. Think of yourself as an industrious person who cannot be distracted by anything negative at the office, as you have legitimate and productive work that needs to be completed, and you just cannot be distracted from accomplishing meaningful goals at your workplace.

What's more, you have just caught the professional colleague, business manager or corporate boss in an office faux pas, as they have made a mistake in playing the corporate game. Maybe you can take advantage of this communication mistake at a later date, but you already have the advantage here by not reacting poorly to the conflict situation.

In this case, you are acting above and beyond what would otherwise be a natural human reaction to the negative communication mistake. Not to mention the fact that the professional colleague, business manager or corporate boss may even feel guilty and internally realize they made a mistake in this scenario.

Human beings are not always perfect in social situations, and you can gain brownie points in the corporate world by acting exceptionally well in extremely negative circumstances. On the grounds that you have every right to respond negatively, but you show considerable restraint and avoid reacting or returning serve in these negative conflict situations.

You will also be admired for having played the game perfectly and exhibiting ideal corporate behavior that is established through decades of professional standards and corporate protocols. In fact, you have just demonstrated the necessary social and behavioral skills that are important for management level positions. Moreover, this exemplary level of professional comportment is on full display for everyone at the office to witness.

Relevantly, others will take note of the professional colleague, business manager or corporate boss and their lack of social and emotional intelligence at the office. The fact that these people should have thought before they acted in such an unprofessional manner will eventually catch up with them in the company.

For example, these people create enemies around the office with this type of improper behavior, and coworkers now have material information which can be used against them in the future. Thus, part of playing the corporate game is not giving your enemies any areas of weakness or material information that can be used against you in a negative fashion.

One can just imagine the conversation when two managers are fighting for the same promotion, and the other competing manager has some material information to utilize in discrediting their main rival for the position. The subtle corporate backstabbing plays out in the following manner, "Well, Jim isn't very good in the area of social and emotional intelligence, he often loses his cool in conversations with subordinates!"

This material information or negative campaigning being reinforced and supported by others around the office through the gossiping process can be the deciding factor in losing a much-coveted promotion. Don't be incredibly naïve at the office, as I can guarantee that your competitors are constantly looking for useful material information or negative campaign details that can be used against you at the company.

So you always ponder and deliberate before you make a move in Corporate America. This helps tremendously in mastering the art of utilizing effective social and emotional intelligence at the office. In point of fact, all the smooth-talking management types usually have this part down pat in their social and behavioral interactions with people in the business community.

These business professionals know every euphemistic phrase in the corporate handbook. They are the masters of phony corporate speak, but that's how you stay out of trouble, avoid the treacherous corporate landmines, and optimally play the game.

"We cannot enter into alliances until we are acquainted with the designs of our neighbors."

In the corporate environment people try to network and build relationships they think will hold strategic value and eventually benefit them in some way. However, spend most of your time when you join a company or move into a new position by performing well in the role and producing good solid work results.

But absolutely stay out of the alliance and networking game. There is plenty of time for that later on, as your primary concern needs to be building a good professional reputation in the new role. The goal is to demonstrate your incredible work ethic, high-level of competency and overall value to colleagues in the department or business unit.

The added benefit is that you can use this time to study those around you carefully because there are a lot of snakes in corporations. Similarly, avoid rushing to judgement in evaluating your business colleagues. Just because a coworker is nice to you, treats you well, and acts like they want to be your friend, doesn't mean they have good intentions in the end. Spend lots of time studying little things that don't seem to add up with your coworkers, as corporations are nothing if they aren't giant repositories of information and sordid gossip machines.

There is so much information floating around about your colleagues, and you are going to have to spend considerable time and effort disentangling the truth from the various falsehoods. There is a lot of incorrect information circulating around the office as a result of jealous agendas and a plethora of interfering busybodies. It is important to separate the facts from the spurious gossip and take to heart the phrase *all that glitters is not gold* in the corporate world.

You will be surprised as you progress through your corporate career to discover just how many coworkers you thought were your friends were actually backstabbing and sabotaging you behind your back at the company. These corporate snakes are so deceptively good that even if a coworker says something like, "Bret, you might want to watch out for Cindy!"

Instead, you think to yourself that Cindy is always extremely helpful and that you have a great working relationship with her at the office. In fact, Cindy seems so competent, supportive, and nice in your personal communications and interactions with her that you find this notice hard to believe. So you respond to the warning, "Nah, Cindy has been really nice to me, she is always very helpful!"

The coworker just shakes their head internally because they know that Cindy has been saying a lot of damaging and negative things about you behind your back. Unfortunately, the coworker will not just come right out and tell you these things. Instead, the coworker tries to give you a subtle hint regarding your colleague's duplicitous behavior behind the scenes. But juxtaposed against Cindy's friendly and helpful behavior towards you directly, and some cryptic warning about her, you simply dismiss the coworker's warning as insignificant corporate white noise.

It so happens that down the line, you come to find out that Cindy was outright sabotaging your career behind the scenes with some pretty devious, malicious, and underhanded backstabbing practices. So pay attention to the little clues, as there are tidbits of information floating around the office that are indicative of typical backstabbing behaviors by colleagues.

In many situations, deliberate backstabbing and sabotaging behaviors are covered up with readymade explanations like, "This was just a simple communication misunderstanding on the project!" These clues are often subtle, but don't take the naïve approach that since your colleagues are nice and seemingly helpful to your face, that they aren't up to serious no good behind your back at the corporation.

After you have studied the lay of the land, then you can start to build some strategically important relationships and alliances at the office, but not until you can weed out the good quality people from the corporate snakes. And just like a Survivor show, there are a lot of corporate snakes who may even try to make calculated alliances with you, which would not be in your best interests at the company.

As a matter of practice, think about being as neutral as Switzerland and avoid being overanxious about making strategic alliances. This is especially true when you don't really know enough about your corporate colleagues to make good informed decisions in this area.

The primary goal is to focus on doing good high-quality work, as the real alliances that matter are built over the course of a long period of time. This plays out in good competent business colleagues recognizing other highly competent and hardworking individuals. In this world, quality bonds, respects, and seeks out similar quality. These are the real strategic alliances to develop and nourish in your corporate career.

In reality the people who are really focused on alliance building and networking are the ones who don't have the requisite skillsets or professional goods. These people aren't particularly competent at their jobs, and this is how they get ahead in the corporate world, it's called the Peter Principle.[32] And trust me when I tell you this, there are a lot of people that are gossiping and scheming all day long at corporations.

This is a full-time job for these individuals, so you want to identify who these people are at the office, and distance yourself from this type of behavior as much as you can,

---

[32] https://en.wikipedia.org/wiki/Peter_principle; https://www.investopedia.com/terms/p/peter-principle.asp

while still being professionally polite at all times in the corporation. In point of fact, you will discover that your business colleagues definitely have some ulterior motives and calculating moves in their corporate game playing repertoires.

This corporate sleight of hand usually happens behind the scenes, so you have a lot to learn in skillfully recognizing and sifting through inconsistent practices, conflicting information, and duplicitous behaviors with respect to your lovely corporate colleagues as you navigate through your professional career.

In essence, you become a quasi-intelligence officer out of necessity in safeguarding your career from the corporate snakes trying to throw you under the bus when it suits their respective needs. Hence, good intelligence gathering along with a skeptically cautious mind and an unwavering professional approach goes a long way in avoiding some of these traps that your coworkers are routinely setting at the office. Yes, this is similar to military intelligence gathering on your allies and enemies in terms of fundamental war strategy. Welcome to the wonderful world of Corporate America!

"It is the unemotional, reserved, calm, detached warrior who wins, not the hothead seeking vengeance and not the ambitious seeker of fortune."

In the course of your corporate career there are going to be plenty of times when you are just emotionally seething on the inside as a result of typical office dramas. For example, a superior goes overboard in pointing out a minor mistake which occurred on a project you were managing at the corporation. This might not even be your fault, as the analyst simply messed up one of the numbers in their spreadsheet. However, you are being reprimanded severely for not checking the analyst's work on the project.

This of course is impossible in practical terms, checking every analyst's work in a large department, not to mention the fact that busy corporate managers are often responsible for overseeing multiple projects and putting out a myriad of departmental fires at the same time.

This is merely a hypothetical example, however, there are many instances where situations at the office are not handled in the best possible manner. There will be cases where people do not act professionally, and this leads to personal feelings getting hurt in the process. It usually means that some kind of corporate pressure is involved, and oftentimes revolving around financial issues. In fact, as corporate profits go down, everyone starts feeling the pressure.

This pressure usually gets passed down the line from the corporate executives to their direct reports and eventually works its way down to the lowest levels within the corporation. Everyone feels the pressure of poor quarterly earnings reports, especially when the company's stock price is falling like a rock. The next thing you know there are all these new projects which filter down to the business units trying to find additional savings, cut costs, improve efficiencies, close deals, increase sales volume, and improve overall performance.

This increased pressure is like a noose which gets tighter the more you struggle, tempers start to rise, and office conflicts start bubbling up to the surface in direct proportion to the amount of pressure that the company is experiencing internally and externally.

The corporate perks are great, as the big companies have the high margins to pay the good salaries and nice bonuses, but this comes along with a fair amount of pressure and stress. When these corporate dramas flare up at the office, and you find yourself in the center of the storm so to speak, it is going to be extremely easy to get caught up in the emotional aspects of the problem situation.

This would be a normal reaction to have from a response standpoint as we are emotional beings who worked hard to land corporate jobs and have invested a lot of emotional sweat equity into our careers.

However, you almost have to be inhuman to successfully work in corporations these days, as this is no place for natural emotional responses to problem situations that frequently occur in this organizational setting. In fact, robots would be ideally suited for working in this inhuman environment, as they have the perfect personality to deal with all the utter nonsense that is so prevalent in this corporate paradigm.

Consequently, when things go sour at the office, and the corporate world is treating you poorly and unfairly, you have to keep your cool regardless of the inhuman circumstances. For instance, just let your boss scream at you like a banshee over some typical office drama, you always come out ahead by staying calm and composed and reacting like a perfectly programmed robot would in this same problem situation.

Many employees react to the hostility by getting angry, you can see this anger building inside of them, the veins start pulsating in their neck, the tone of their voice changes, and inevitably they say something to the boss which makes the problem situation significantly worse.

Alternatively, these employees become so intensely apoplectic with internal rage, that once the boss leaves, they continue to cogitate over the conflict event with such furiously raw emotions that they cannot concentrate on work at all. This just increases the pressure for the employee because now they are not getting their work done on top of the conflict issue which prompted them to become angry and upset in the first place.

You have to play the long game in Corporate America, you really have to envision this process as a marathon and not a sprint. The employees who cannot control their emotions in the face of office dramas, which there are countless office dramas in every business unit, are going to have a hard time in this corporate world. How you react to these office dramas and problem situations is something that you can absolutely control as a corporate professional.

I am telling you in advance to be prepared for these office dramas because they are inevitable in every corporation on the planet, and probably even exist in other galaxies throughout the universe when you think about it. Nevertheless, how you react to these problem situations is entirely up to you, and this is one of the few things that you can actually control in the corporate world. Therefore, reacting well to office dramas and problem situations is one of your primary responsibilities as a successful corporate professional.

Most people react poorly to these office dramas, and it really hurts their corporate careers. In fact, this poor handling of problem situations is probably the single largest factor in people looking for new jobs. Ironically, these people are still going to encounter office dramas and problem situations in their new jobs and companies.

However, they will be starting all over again from square one at the next professional port of call. Furthermore, people tend to repeat the same mistakes over and over again as they move from corporation to corporation, and they wonder why their corporate careers aren't advancing the way they intended.

The other option is to leave the corporate world altogether and do something like drive a semi-trailer truck across the country or find some alternative career by reinventing yourself.

The irony is that one of the reasons people go to college is to get a good paying job in the corporate world. Hence, leaving the corporate career behind is a step that shouldn't be taken lightly. Nevertheless, many people do quit their corporate careers because they couldn't handle the pressure of office dramas or learn the skills necessary for handling these difficult problem situations in the workplace.

Instead of recognizing their shortcomings in this area and working on developing better game playing strategies and techniques to handle these difficult problem situations at the office, many people keep using the same ineffectual approach that burns a lot of bridges in the corporate world.

These people almost stubbornly refuse to learn the rules of the corporate game, and continually make things worse by not properly controlling their emotions and behaviors, and this ultimately has decidedly negative consequences for their corporate careers.

These emotional and behavioral shortcomings can play out in a number of non-productive and unprofessional outcomes. It will never help your corporate career to openly disagree with the human resources representative, become angry with a business colleague, argue with a coworker, and escalate tensions with your boss or manager. Once this happens in the workplace, you have already lost the corporate game. There is definitely a behavioral and philosophical mindset which can help you compete better in the corporate world.

You literally have to think with a Zen-like mindset where you always achieve and maintain this calm, imperturbable state at the office. This rational state of mind, where one is distinctly detached from the viscerally unfiltered emotional state confers an advantage by bringing an analytic clarity and mental focus to approaching and solving these complex office dramas and problem situations in the corporate world.

There is always some emergency that is occurring at the business unit level or within the company as a whole, it is almost like a corporate law of nature. There is constantly some mess that needs to be cleaned up or some fire that needs to be put out in the corporate world. It is commonplace to have this, *we have to do this right now* mentality, and *everything is riding on this deal* kind of pressurized corporate culture which generates enormous amounts of stress and tension in the workplace.

Ironically, most of this unnecessary drama and pressure is self-imposed aggravation by the very people in positions of authority within the company. This is mainly due to the fact that corporations are poorly managed and incompetently run business operations these days, especially in America.

Frequently, the leadership team cannot competently and properly handle problem situations, so the natural response is simply to propagate the pressure and stress onto everyone else around them at the company. In the corporate world, every action almost certainly has a reaction, and in many cases it is quite negative, in an almost deferential bow to Newtonian physics.

At any rate, these action-reaction functions usually spiral out of control until someone ultimately becomes collateral damage within the corporation. This is followed by human resources and upper management trying to put the best possible spin on the unfavorable chain of events from an internal marketing standpoint.

The company also seeks to mitigate the inevitable fallout that results from these office dramas and problem situations going awry. And when you find yourself in one of these office dramas and problem situations, the best way to approach these incidents is by maintaining a Zen-like state of mind and keeping your emotions in check at all times.

There will always be someone at the company who cannot mentally handle the pressure and stress of the corporate environment, and this is generally reflected in them losing control of their emotions. In a sense, these individuals become the sacrificial lambs of the corporation.

The goal is to stay calm in the maelstrom of emotions that inevitably arise from these intense office dramas and problem situations at the corporation. The individuals who maintain a calm and rational state of mind while everyone else is losing their cool, are the victors in the corporate game.

I would like to make a point here regarding the notion of revenge at the office. For instance, if you have been wronged by colleagues at the company, don't have the mindset that you need to seek revenge against these people. Just be above all this petty revenge nonsense, as you are being distracted from your primary objectives of doing high quality work and adding measurable value to the corporation.

There are several Western philosophers like Francis Bacon and Friedrich Nietzsche who discuss the idea of revenge in their works.[33] This philosophical thinking promotes the idea that the better path is to avoid getting caught up and obsessed with all this small-minded pettiness and vindictiveness which revolves around the practice of seeking revenge.

It is much more beneficial in life to avoid fixating and focusing on the past, be above it all, and move on with your life. Instead, use this same mental energy towards more positive endeavors and high-yielding pursuits like being more productive at work, developing your career, and improving your physical and mental well-being.

It is apparent that corporations are full of wronged people and a revenge seeking mentality. There are far too many people in corporations these days wasting valuable time plotting and seeking their revenge. These people are endlessly obsessing over some office drama where they were wronged by coworkers, to the point that this entirely consumes all their thoughts and behaviors in life.

This just isn't the best approach to take as a life strategy.

---

[33] https://plato.stanford.edu/entries/francis-bacon/; https://plato.stanford.edu/entries/nietzsche/

The reasoning here, is that you lose the first time by getting wronged, and then you lose the second time by wasting all this energy and mental resources thinking about being wronged.

This is entirely unhealthy for you as a human being, as getting upset and cogitating over these issues of revenge leads to additional negative outcomes like sleepless nights, an assortment of health problems, and wasted time and energy that could be better utilized towards more fruitful endeavors in life. Therefore, avoid falling into the revenge trap at the corporation.

Sometimes you just have to take responsibility for the fact that your opponents played the game better than you at the office. Just acknowledge the fact that your opponents got the best of you in this particular game. Take it as a lesson learned and move on, but don't lose twice by destroying yourself in the process of seeking revenge. This is because more often than not, it just isn't worth it to pursue the strategy of plotting revenge in the corporate world.

The thoughts of revenge seeking and trying to get even with your opponents, means you probably need to do some more work on controlling your emotions, and learning to take a Zen-like approach towards your corporate career and overall life. For instance, if you are regularly giving drivers the middle finger who cut you off in traffic, there is just a better way of controlling your emotions. The takeaway here is that you need to get much better in this area of disciplined self-control.

Just be above all this nonsense and move on with your much larger and important goals in life and the corporate world. Don't waste any more time getting angry over some of these stupid, small-minded, and incredibly insecure people you encounter at the office. In most cases, these small-minded people are just not worth getting upset over, as they simply cannot help themselves regarding the way they think and behave at the corporation.

The last part of the Sun Tzu quote with reference to "the ambitious seeker of fortune" is still very applicable today. Just focus on doing high-quality work and trying to bring substantial value to the positions you are given within the corporation. Enjoy the journey, as good work has its own rewards. Avoid having the mindset where you are always chasing the next promotion and looking for the big corporate payoff.

In reality, only a handful of people at smaller companies make the crazy money. And at larger companies there are more people who can have sizable incomes, but nevertheless, only an extremely small percentage of employees as a whole are going to make insane amounts of money working in the corporate world.

This being said, the total compensation packages at corporations puts these workers on the upper end of the income distribution scale in the United States and the world as a whole. In point of fact, corporate employees as a group have it rather good when you start looking at the broad view of total compensation and overall work environment. For instance, corporate employees are not working in the hot sun or a cold and damp warehouse for twelve hours a day.

The important role of corporate employees should not be underestimated, as they form the backbone of a reliable tax base which provides extensive support for local communities. The corporate employees also serve as the foundation in supporting entire ecosystems within the community.

These community employment sectors and services include childcare, education, churches, housing, healthcare, laundry, house cleaning, landscaping, home repairs, transportation, retail, restaurants, entertainment, and commercial real estate. These symbiotic relationships thrive within the community ecosystem as a result of corporate employees being at the top of the employment food chain.

This economic supply chain receives a big boost from these nice paying corporate jobs which spreads the wealth in the surrounding community. This is why cities and states try so hard to attract large companies to their particular region of the country through corporate tax breaks.

The big corporations make enormous amounts of money, have high margins, and pay good salaries to their employees. These companies also infuse local communities with lots of capital and economic stimulus which sustains a healthy ecosystem of business commerce.

The larger point being made here is that the combination of corporate benefits, good salaries, company perks, and comfortable working environment make corporate careers worthwhile pursuits. These corporate careers are greatly beneficial in achieving a high standard of living and an overall good quality of life.

Fundamentally, a corporate job is a nice job to have all things being equal. So focus on doing excellent work at the office, learn to derive enjoyment from the process of developing your corporate skillset, and you will have more than enough financial resources to live a good, high quality life.

In summary, worry about continually learning new things at the office, strive to constantly develop the tools in your corporate toolbox, and in the end, the money will take care of itself. As in, nobody who is any good, has ever complained about not making enough money in Corporate America! Hence, your primary goal is to become good, and develop yourself as a corporate asset that has marketable value.

If all your doing is chasing the crazy money in Corporate America, then you will likely be disappointed. Moreover, this approach could possibly interfere with you reaching your goal in the end anyway.

By way of illustration, I remember in the seventh grade all the other kids were so worried about being first team starters on the football team. On the other hand, I was just trying to do good in practice every day with no expectations at all, and hopefully have the opportunity to play on the second team.

I wasn't thinking about anything else except what was right in front of me each day at football practice. So it came as a pleasant surprise when the coaches made me a first team starter, especially considering that I was one of the smaller players on the football team.

The moral of the story is don't get distracted by outside forces which inevitably take your eye off the ball. Avoid being overly concerned with chasing the money in the corporate world, as this means you probably aren't addressing the very things required to get the money in the first place, funny how that works isn't it. By focusing so much on a potential outcome which really has extraordinarily little to do with what it takes to get that outcome, you are really doing yourself a disservice.

In fact, obsessing over the very outcome that you desire, may lead you to act and behave in a manner which denies yourself that very goal. For instance, think in terms of typical pursuits like chasing happiness, self-interest, and money. Instead of focusing so much on the end result or final outcome, learn to enjoy the process and the journey along the way towards achieving your long-term goals and aspirations in both the corporate world and in life.

I am not a Buddhist, or even a Zen Buddhist for that matter. I view the world through the prism of Materialism, but religions often have useful principles and insights concerning human behavior that are beneficial to people and society.

Accordingly, in my travels through the world of Corporate America, having a Zen-like approach and mindset in this environment is a good way to conduct oneself as a corporate professional. This Zen-like approach will definitely help you achieve better results at the office and play the corporate game more effectively.

I am not going to break down every Sun Tzu quote and show you the relevance to the corporate environment, that isn't the goal here. I am just trying to get you to think about concepts, ideas, and situations with these philosophical principles and strategies in mind.

As I can substantiate from personal experience, the corporate environment has a lot in common with military conquests from a strategy standpoint. I started to notice these similarities when thinking deeply about office dramas and problem situations that routinely come up in Corporate America.

In analyzing these events in detail, I would often fall back on many of the strategic principles laid out in Sun Tzu quotes. I concluded that the information being expressed in these Sun Tzu quotes is still quite relevant today. These quotes are full of impactful ideas and represent an effective tool in managing many of these difficult office dramas and problem situations that regularly occur in the corporate world.

So just go to many online resources that break down quotes from The Art of War, or better yet, just buy a good translation of the book on Amazon. It isn't like you need to learn Chinese or the book costs a fortune to buy in the marketplace. The goal here is to start thinking conceptually about strategy on a much deeper level than most people do as a course of habit.

This is the primary goal, and not necessarily to run your corporate career as a military campaign via the principles of Sun Tzu's philosophy. But rather to think deeper about the various strategies and options available to you when determining the best course of action for managing a problem situation at the office.

Some of the best and most straightforward takeaways

from the quotes and military thinking of Sun Tzu, is in outlining what not to do from a strategy standpoint.

Likewise, when thinking deeply about corporate game theory, you will start to realize that there are some definite actions and behaviors or military strategies to avoid in the corporate world. Just learning what not to do can give you a substantial advantage over your business colleagues and competitors in this corporate environment. Many a corporate career has been built on just avoiding the stupid mistakes that trip up so many people at the office.

And finally, knowing what to do at all times is undoubtedly a more difficult challenge, as in a lot of cases it depends, and this is the next level of strategic thinking. However, just start with mastering the easy stuff, as when you replay office dramas and problem situations in your head, I am sure you can recognize there are some specific corporate strategies that work in most cases. Just mastering these corporate strategies that work under most scenarios can go a long way towards keeping you out of serious trouble and staying in the game as a viable player.

It is important to remember that many of your business colleagues are going to fall by the wayside, as half the battle in Corporate America is just staying in the game and outlasting your competition. Oftentimes it simply comes down to which players make the least mistakes in the corporate world. At heart, the corporate world really is a war of attrition. Thus, I am sure Sun Tzu would feel right at home in the present day playing the corporate game.

11 THE CORPORATE GAME

In this chapter we discuss the manner in which you present yourself at the office, as in what character you are playing in the game. The reason this is important in the overall scope of the corporate game, is that how you carry yourself at the office, basically sets the ground rules for how you are going to be treated by others in the corporation. You are telling your coworkers and management how you expect and want to be treated, whether you realize it or not.

Some people are their own worst enemy, and they are actually subconsciously sabotaging themselves at the office. These people make themselves ideal candidates for problematical outcomes by the way they act and behave in the corporate world. If you are regularly being disrespected, treated poorly, given bad projects, not being promoted, incessantly criticized, and not taken seriously at the office, then maybe you are presenting the wrong image to your business colleagues and managers.

It is important to take ownership and responsibility for how you comport yourself at all times within the corporation, as people in general are so quick to blame others for their plight in life. Sometimes a little self-evaluation and introspection is in order to realize what role you are playing in eliciting certain types of behavioral responses towards you by colleagues and management within the corporation.

It is important to note that there are definitely office bullies in the corporate world. It may be more subtle than the types we encountered in school growing up, but the bullying behaviors exist in the comfortable corridors of Corporate America, and you need to protect yourself from these corporate hyenas.

I am not one who takes advantage of other people's weaknesses just because I recognize them, and others take this approach as well, but unfortunately there are enough people in the workplace environment who do this very practice, that you need to protect yourself from the office predators so to speak.

It is quite apparent that human beings are not as nice as greeting cards would suggest, and there are a lot of people in the corporate world who for a multitude of reasons will attack other people's deficiencies and personal weaknesses.

Any weakness they find in the other person at the office, they will pick it like a scab. Usually these office predators are highly insecure people deep down inside, or just very unhappy individuals at the core. In many cases, these corporate hyenas are just plain petty and small-minded by nature.

One experiences the same type of insecure people and small-minded behavior at every level in society. For example, this predatory behavior is prevalent in grade schools, high schools, colleges, prisons, churches, social organizations, and even liberal-minded corporations.

Meanwhile in Corporate America, there inevitably exists this kind of subtle bullying, intimidation, and power dynamic which is being exploited in the strategic playing of the game. Moreover, every corporate employee and calculating game player factors this stark reality into their decision-making process at the office.

There is still some blatant bullying and openly mean-spirited behavior occurring in the corporate world, but these are usually very isolated incidents because this approach creates a lot of ammunition for opponents to use against the corporate bully. As a result, there is much less of this type of blatant bullying behavior in the more sophisticated company cultures these days. However, this just means people are smarter and stealthier in their methods of treating others at the office very poorly and in an unprofessional manner.

There is definitely an abundance of subtly disrespectful behavior occurring daily at the typical office in Corporate America, and this ultimately causes a lot of sleepless nights for stressed out corporate employees. For instance, there are sophisticated ways of cutting people down, talking condescendingly to them, undermining their overall confidence and self-esteem, and treating them as incapable human beings. There are also clever methods to downplay the achievements and contributions of corporate employees and negatively impact their future prospects for career advancement.

One of the most subtle but yet highly destructive behaviors in Corporate America, is that of gossiping behind the scenes about coworkers, effectively discrediting their character, work ethic and overall competency in the process. This pernicious and distasteful behavior is in essence a negative marketing campaign which lowers the perceived value within the corporation of the targeted individual.

There are similarly subtle ways to diminish the influence and opportunities for corporate employees by excluding them from important conversations and high-visibility meetings, belittling their accomplishments at work, and throwing them under the bus whenever possible with the goal of ruining their corporate reputation.

These types of sabotaging behaviors may fly under the radar compared to the overt predatory bullying practices which everyone can witness firsthand, but the effects are still quite devastating for those involved. This extremely subtle way of treating employees very poorly and in an unfair manner happens more than human resources and upper management will ever acknowledge publicly at corporations.

These negative behaviors and practices are often quite vicious in nature and have serious consequences for corporate careers. In fact, the corporate environment can be quite stressful and upsetting to employees who find themselves easy targets for these kinds of poor behavioral practices by their stealthily sabotaging corporate colleagues.

The corporations are aware of what I refer to as this corporate snake behavior, and they do pay lip service to the issue somewhat via company sponsored propagandist communication materials. In theory, the corporations hope to brainwash their poor behaving employees by promoting sacred corporate values and wishing to instill this idealistic environment where everyone is happy and respectful for others at the office.

The companies expect to bring about this miracle of humanity through nicely produced training videos, corporate value posters, educational classes, and internal communication materials. However, this corporate utopian dream seems to be a perpetually lost cause when juxtaposed against the nasty inclinations of human nature.

In reality, corporate environments are ideal breeding grounds for this vicious backstabbing mentality which is so prevalent in the corporate world. In fact, human beings really seem to crave or ultimately devolve into the baser aspects of human behavior while working at corporations.

Given that we are trying to navigate the real world of Corporate America, and not the idealistic dream world portrayed via a human resources inspired corporate values poster. This means that you need to take actions to protect yourself and proactively ward off some of this untoward behavior by coworkers at the office. As human resources waiving a magical wand isn't going to make this nasty and malicious behavior go away anytime soon in the corporate world.

Even if you have a great office culture, where everyone is very respectful towards others in the company, you are still broadcasting information and behavioral messages about yourself to colleagues at the office. In this information which your coworkers are deciphering and interpreting, is essentially the blueprint for how they are going to react and treat you in these social and behavioral relationships at work.

Therefore, you want to present the greatest possible image which will help you compete successfully and be treated optimally in these behavioral and social transactions within the corporation. This great image is critical in working on the high-visibility projects, creating an individual brand, competing for coveted positions, being successfully promoted, and ultimately having a more productive and rewarding career in the corporate world.

This is all part of playing the corporate game, and you can bet that your competitors are either naturally good at presenting the right image which helps market themselves ideally, or they have worked really hard, taken advice from mentors, and spent considerable time creating, branding, and performing the role of this behavioral persona which represents the best possible vehicle for promoting their corporate careers.

One may believe that you are etched in stone from a personality standpoint, and that you either couldn't alter how you present yourself at the office, or you are above this particular strategy, and you will just let your work do the talking. Well, this isn't going to change the fact that others are still going to treat you accordingly, and you are making things much harder for yourself in the workplace. Hence, you have to deal with the consequences of this individual choice and game playing strategy.

Ultimately, we are responsible and accountable for our lot in life. This is a case where we can add real value and maintain a level of control over how we present ourselves in the corporate world, so we might as well exercise some proactive planning in this area.

Now that we have aptly defined the real world of corporate relationships and behaviors, you need to ask yourself, what kind of image am I presenting to my colleagues at the office? How did you first present yourself when you joined the company? You know what they say about first impressions!

How do you think others view you in the corporation? What personality characteristics do you display for your public persona at the workplace? How do you spend your free time at the office? Do you go to lunch with a group of people or do you eat alone at your desk and in the breakroom? Are you regarded as a helpful or selfish person in the corporation when it comes to supporting others? Whether you realize it or not, you have created a specific image and distinct persona for yourself at the corporation.

There are many instances where you are sending signals to business colleagues and advertising your brand image. For example, do you bring donuts to the department on Fridays? Are you participating in company office pools and fantasy leagues with your coworkers? Do you dress really well? What is your style: casual, business casual, business formal or business professional?[34] How do you style your hair and wear makeup? Do you smack your gum, or wear heavy perfume and cologne?

All these things say something about you to colleagues in the corporate world. It isn't good enough to just have a personal style and come what may. You will get come what

---

[34] https://www.moneycrashers.com/what-wear-work-tips-office-dress-code/

may reactions and results at the office, and this is no way to cultivate a professionally positive corporate image and play the game in an optimal manner.

This is serious business here, as we are talking about critical promotions and all-important money. For instance, if you are going to put up with all the nonsense that goes into working in Corporate America, then you might as well get paid the better salaries for essentially working in the same stressful environment.

It is imperative to be self-aware at the office. I witnessed business colleagues who routinely had bad breath after lunch in the corporate setting, and it was really bad. It is crucial to know these types of things about yourself, and if you like to eat sushi for lunch, then brush your teeth and take breath mints after eating. And you wonder why nobody wants to talk to you after lunch!

In summary, be introspective of the behaviors and branding image that you present to others at the office because you essentially get back what you put out there from a behavioral, personal image, and overall persona standpoint.

You are always on display at the office and being sized up as a colleague, competitor, and person. Human beings categorize things naturally, as they put everyone they meet into little groupings and classification systems.

This is an evolutionary useful tool which provides practical value to human beings in navigating the complex world of behavioral and social relationships. Accordingly, business professionals put their coworkers into categories to decide how they should best react and treat these people in the workplace.

So help them classify you as a winner in the corporate world. Ideally, you should be thought of as the consummate professional who is a talented and hardworking employee. You need to be perceived as a smart and knowledgeable individual who is polite and respectful of others in the organization. In short, a valuable asset and resource worth protecting and promoting within the company.

In contrast, don't let your business colleagues categorize you as a loser in the corporate world. Avoid being viewed as careless, lazy, incompetent, old, out of touch, stupid, and simple-minded as a corporate professional. Don't get classified as being non-managerial material, especially if you have managerial aspirations for your career.

You want to avoid being negatively labeled by business colleagues and upper management in your company. For instance, you can be older in terms of actual years without being viewed as old in the negative connotative sense of the characterization, if you know what I mean.

Do you carry yourself as an experienced, sharp, and vibrant professional or do you grumble all day at work about how old you are getting? Do you embrace learning new technology or are you constantly complaining about learning new software systems, and giving the impression that technology has really passed you by in the modern corporation? You get the picture here, as a lot of this is personal branding. It often comes down to how you package and present yourself in the corporate world, as the very same core entity can be packaged with an entirely different branding strategy.

You need to think about your branding strategy for playing the game in the corporate world. If you think this isn't that important, then you are giving your competitors a huge advantage in the game.

Why do you think advertising agencies and marketing firms get paid so much money to brand and package products to consumers? This is because advertising and marketing campaigns do an excellent job of branding and differentiating products in the market.

There are innumerable examples such as the Marlboro Man to sell cigarettes, the Apple logo to sell technology products, and everything else under the sun from marketing bottled water to promoting political candidates.

These businesses all understand the importance and value of branding, marketing, and packaging their products. You are a product in the corporate market whether you recognize it or not. You are marketing and selling yourself every day at the office, you are in essence, your own brand manager. So think about how you want to portray your image and market your persona in the workplace because you are continuously being categorized, evaluated, and judged by everyone around you on a daily basis.

Here are some of the typical character types at the office. I will start with the gregarious, poorly dressed, overweight jokester who is always chatting, telling great stories, extremely friendly, a natural-born extrovert, and the life of the department. However, this person is not viewed as overly ambitious, competent, or hardworking as an employee. This type of corporate persona is not well respected by upper management, and not considered as a good candidate for additional responsibilities and further promotions within the company.

If you fit in this category, then start going on a diet and lose some weight. It would be a good idea to begin exercising regularly and take additional pride in your personal appearance. For instance, get some new clothes that fit your physique well and start dressing in a much more business serious manner. You can still be social, but cut back on the frivolous office conversations, as you don't have to be the life of the party.

It would also be beneficial for your image transformation to begin working overtime on important projects with the goal of impressing your boss and business colleagues through your newfound work ethic. If the change in behavior is noticeable, then your coworkers will think you are turning over a new leaf at the company. In your mind, envisage the idea of displaying a sharp, competent, and ambitious image to upper management.

The goal here is to create the necessary image and corporate persona so that you can be considered for future higher responsibility roles within the organization.

Another character type is the serious professional who is extremely hardworking and practically lives at the office. These individuals are no-nonsense, extremely ambitious, and avoid wasting time on frivolous activities like gossiping or discussing their personal problems during the workday.

The aforementioned are all business as their main purpose during the workday is to accomplish great things and complete projects in an efficient manner. In practice, these individuals are always on the move and rarely have time for small talk.

Above all, these employees are viewed as ambitious, competent, and hardworking by their business colleagues and upper management. As a result, these corporate professionals are considered movers in the company and perceived internally as the likely candidates for extra responsibilities and future promotions.

The downside of this corporate persona is that these individuals can come across as a little too cold, ambitious, and calculating. Oftentimes, these corporate professionals are perceived by others at the office as being unfriendly, selfish, and unsociable.

The biggest problem for these people is they are advertising to higher ranking personnel in the organization that they are a competitive threat for them and their respective positions. In fact, the austerely serious and dedicated professional often develops enemies along the way who feel endangered by their overall presence, competency level, and highly competitive spirit within the corporation.

Unsurprisingly, these individuals open themselves up as likely targets for career sabotage by higher ranking personnel, essentially wanting to keep them down on the corporate ladder. Human beings will resort to some rather nasty behaviors when they feel threatened in a competitive game playing environment.

If you fit in this category, then soften up your personality and demeanor a little bit. Seek to have some occasionally frivolous and lighthearted conversations, making time to be friendly and saying hello to everyone at the office with a warm smile. Even though you are really ambitious and looking for your next promotion opportunity at the company, present less of an obvious and overly ambitious corporate persona to business colleagues and upper management. Just make your overall image appear warmer and less standoffish in nature.

One of your primary goals in the corporate world is to be as humble as possible, especially around managers and executives above your pay scale. In all respects, try not to present an image where they view you as a threat or direct competitor. Even though you might very well be a threat to them, don't advertise this fact, and just hide in plain sight so to speak. It is wise to sneak up on your competition at the office as much as possible, similarly to the sport of American football, where the defense tries to disguise their coverage scheme against their opponent in the game.

In truth, every employee is going to need the help of superiors to move up the corporate ladder, so make them feel comfortable in promoting you. Indeed, present the image that you will serve as another extension of their power base in the corporation. Try to convey the idea that because you are so admiring of them as managers and executives, that your promotion only helps these corporate benefactors consolidate more power in the organization. Ideally, you want to communicate the belief that you will always have the interests of your superiors in mind while playing the corporate game. Thus, these superiors gain by promoting you into more powerful positions within the company.

You need to be viewed as an ally, the proverbial wolf in sheep's clothing. You don't want the entire office to know that you are a wolf, this just makes it extremely hard to play the corporate game. You keep pulling this magic trick off, hiding in plain sight, all the way to the top of the organization. All the while, convincing your colleagues and superiors that you have their best interests at heart in making strategic moves when playing the corporate game.

In this approach, you are never creating a threatening image to the other competitors in the game who are clearly seeking more power for themselves. And make no mistake, moving up the corporate ladder is a competition in every sense of the word.

You are the best friend and devoted ally of your superiors, as you are there to serve the needs and interests of these people at all times. Just think in terms of a dog's level of personal loyalty and fidelity here, one that is never in question. Again, the idea here is that you create an implicit understanding with these managers and executives, that in promoting you, they are essentially furthering their own interests within the corporation.

In essence, these superiors are helping to insulate themselves from future attacks by competitors within the organization. This is because they now have you as an ally in a key position which fortifies their rear flank to some extent. One should keep in mind, this book discusses a lot of corporate game theory for a reason, as these types of chess moves and strategic maneuvers are quite common in the corporate world.

The next character type to discuss is the quiet mousy analyst, who is shy with truly little in the way of people skills. These individuals are good in their roles, but not viewed as leader types within the corporation.

This isn't necessarily that bad of an image or corporate persona for the analyst role, and these people do seem to escape a lot of the typical office drama and mean-spirited politics on balance.

Even more so if they are really good at their job, this is a much-needed function, and nobody really likes doing the work because it is overly tedious or highly technical in nature. Hence, avoiding much of the classic office drama and stressful workplace politics is always a nice outcome and worthy benefit derived from one's corporate persona.

However, the downside of this corporate persona is that this person is likely going to be categorized as a career analyst and essentially working in the same role for 30 years at corporations. This isn't the end of the world, as career senior analysts make relatively good money and can have lengthy corporate careers. An additional benefit is they can handle most projects during regular business hours, leaving them plenty of time for discovering enjoyment and satisfaction in hobbies and interests outside of work.

The difficult part is that many of these analysts want more than being career analysts with no upward mobility, as they want to be promoted to managerial roles just like everyone else in the corporation. And to be candid, being a manager is a whole lot more fun all things being equal than toiling over spreadsheets and databases all day long.

If you fit in this category, then break out of your analyst shell for goodness' sake. Start getting involved with committees, planning groups, cultural societies, and other organizations that your company sponsors for various purposes. Begin networking through these social activities and corporate events with the goal of meeting new contacts, improving your people skills, and opening yourself up to further mentoring possibilities.

This will force you to get out there and mingle in these corporate activities which are outside of your normal comfort zone and core competencies. If you can get important positions on committees to plan and schedule events for your organizational members, then this would be a meaningful step in the right direction. This is all meant to demonstrate and market the fact that you have distinct leadership skills and managerial capabilities which go unnoticed in your current role within the company.

It is worth noting that while you are getting more experience from pushing yourself into these challenging new social and behavioral situations and acquiring additional leadership responsibilities within the corporation. This personal awakening and discovery process should also positively lead to further self-belief and improved overall confidence in your abilities as a corporate professional.

The goal is to rebrand yourself at the corporation. Think of doing things at the office regarding how you carry yourself which are contrary to the mousy analyst stereotype that just wants to be left alone to work quietly in the corner.

This rebranding process involves actively engaging and seeking out conversations and meetings with other business colleagues and superiors to learn more about different parts of the organization. This creates the image of an ambitious employee wanting to learn different facets of the business by examining and studying corporate processes, overall best practices, and accumulating organizational knowledge.

All of this purposeful rebranding activity is intended to present an image of an upwardly mobile corporate professional who is constantly developing and learning as an asset within the corporation. You are actively marketing the corporate persona of an ambitious employee who has the required work ethic, diverse skillset, and corporate mindset for being more than simply a career analyst with the company. The point here is that upper management has to start viewing you as managerial material, and not too meek and quiet to lead a group, department, and business unit. In short, changing the mousy analyst type perception.

It is also important to learn everything about all the parts within your direct area of expertise in the organization. It is a distinct advantage to know your department, corporate function, and overall business unit inside and out.

The objective is to fully understand every technological system, all the essential business processes, and core responsibilities of everyone in the department. This helps you present the image of a knowledgeable go-to person for solving problems and resolving issues that arise in the department.

This knowledge-based expertise creates an image of authority which offers innumerable opportunities to step outside of your mousy persona and show real leadership skills in resolving thorny issues and complicated problems that occur in the company. This expertise provides you with visibility and a platform, so take full advantage of these opportunities to shine in the spotlight.

In some respects you may not be seen as the ideal management type from a personality standpoint. However, if you know the departmental processes better than anyone else in the company, then who better to manage the function when your boss is promoted or leaves the company.

This is another way to position yourself for a managerial promotion by presenting a knowledge-based leadership image at the office. This branding strategy accentuates your positive attributes while also minimizing your inherent managerial weaknesses as a candidate. Truly more than one mousy analyst type has moved into a managerial role through this very game playing strategy.

In moving on to the next character type we commonly find in the corporation. There is the overachieving employee who is always available to help, no matter what the request, and gets along with everyone at the office. The veritable little busy bee which represents the model employee and seems to be created in a human resources lab.

These are unique creatures in the corporate world who

appear to be plugged into their own electrical energy outlets. Oftentimes these individuals are relatively fresh out of college which would explain the high energy levels, but I have seen business professionals with 20 years of experience behind them maintain this busy bee approach and can-do attitude towards getting things done at the office.

This is not a bad image to cultivate at the office, because there is a lot of work to be done, and someone who helps out on all sorts of projects and gets along with everyone is an asset in the corporation. However, be aware that this is the image and persona you are portraying to business colleagues and upper management within the company.

Some of the downside to this persona is that business colleagues and upper management often take advantage of these individuals in a number of ways. For instance, to complete their unfinished tasks, do the dirty work that nobody wants, and take on ad hoc projects which make other people look good in the end. Again, remember about the image you present at the office, as it tells others how to treat you from a behavioral standpoint.

This might be the reason you feel deep down inside that you are being used and taken advantage of at the corporation. Especially if you are overly eager to solve all the problems and clean up the messes of your coworkers at the office.

Furthermore, because you are presenting this busy bee corporate persona which is there to serve the needs and interests of your coworkers, this brand image often gets grouped and categorized into the subordinate classification system. Right alongside the secretarial and working group levels from a categorization perspective in the minds of upper management. In addition, this personality type can be pigeonholed as a bit of a simpleton, and not really regarded as a deep strategist when it comes to overall business theory.

All that being said, this is still such a good corporate persona in so many respects that it is hard to fault any employee for adopting this game playing strategy. This persona has a lot of redeeming qualities that are net positives for these individuals, and in many cases are quite helpful in being promoted into higher responsibility roles within the corporation. It really depends upon what upper management values and promotes in a given company. Afterall, who doesn't like a smart busy bee that gets a lot accomplished at the office.

In order to mitigate some of the negative aspects of this persona, avoid coming across as an overeager muttonhead that just says yes to anything at the office, no matter the absurdity of the project request. Always keep the big picture in mind and demonstrate that you are recognizing and understanding the bigger picture when going around doing all these busy bee activities. Moreover, make sure that you are doing as much purposeful work with your time as possible, and not just being a busy bee for busy bee's sake. Otherwise, business colleagues and upper management will give you less credit for all your hard work.

And finally, demonstrate good leadership qualities and skills by delegating and finding other future busy bees around the office to help work on some of your ad hoc and external project requests. If practicable, put whole teams together of other busy bees from different departments to spread the workload around in getting these special projects done which are outside of your formal job scope.

This ability to organize, motivate, and lead informal groups where colleagues volunteer to work together on your busy bee projects shows real leadership abilities. This definitely presents the proper brand image regarding strong management material for senior people in the organization. This is invariably how you play the game and get ahead in the corporate world.

The last character type we will discuss in this chapter is the classic slacker persona in the corporation. This individual does the bare minimum to keep their job and sets the bar incredibly low regarding expectations around the office. This person routinely has a bunch of ignored or unanswered emails in their Outlook mailbox and does almost everything half-ass in a low competency manner.

Obviously, this slacker persona is going to cause the employee considerable pushback and problems at the office. So if this isn't who you are as a corporate professional, but you are doing things at the office which can be perceived along these lines, then you definitely want to make some changes in your behavioral branding style.

First and foremost, make sure that you get to work on time every day, and if possible, make it in early to the office most days of the week. Spend the first part of the morning clearing out your Outlook mailbox and making sure that you are well-organized with an action plan for being highly productive at work each day.

Another way that you can change your brand image in the corporation is to start working overtime at the office and bringing your laptop home to put in more hours during the workweek. Everyone pays attention to who is consistently working nights and weekends in the company. It is important to work a little harder than your previous standard with regard to work ethic, so that business colleagues and upper management notice and recognize this change in behavior.

In addition, create extra value on the projects that you are responsible for delivering by exceeding expectations in a meaningful and quantifiable manner. And when others ask you for help regarding their project issues and have special requests, make timely meetings to go over these items, and present a real team-friendly approach towards your coworkers in the organization.

Do the quality of work which exemplifies going the

extra mile on projects that you are responsible for working on, and make sure you are highly organized and have planned the entire project in a thorough manner covering all practical contingencies. Furthermore, take pride in doing things at a high level of competency at the office, from dressing sharply and exhibiting excellent communication skills, to having a neat workspace and making efficient use of your time.

Sometimes a lack of training or skillset deficiencies can make an employee look like a corporate slacker. If you have some skillset deficiencies in an area like software, systems and technology which makes you seem incompetent, then proactively address this shortcoming.

Either ask your boss for additional training, take available educational and training courses offered through your company, or go online and complete the necessary classes on your own time. You need to do whatever it takes to address your skillset deficiencies and improve your overall competency levels as an employee in the corporation.

If you really are the classic corporate slacker, and you are happy and content with this particular brand image, along with the subsequent consequences of this corporate persona, then keep playing the game utilizing this same suboptimal strategy.

This isn't the end of the world, as there are many corporate slackers who seem to do just enough to squeak by each year and have 10-year careers in Corporate America. In fact, there are even some corporate employees who have completely mastered all the subtle nuances of this slacker strategy to an ultimate perfection. Just realize that people in the corporate world, namely your boss, business colleagues and upper management will treat you accordingly.

The idea expressed in this chapter is to understand that things don't happen in a complete vacuum. In part we are responsible and play a collaborative role in how others perceive us, and ultimately in how they decide to go about treating us as human beings. Within the framework that the corporate world is really just an extension and manifestation of how human beings interact with each other in a complex social and behavioral environment.

Consequently, instead of spending so much time blaming others for how we are treated at the office, we might benefit from some introspective analysis and thinking, and determine how to present a better brand image in the corporate world.

You need to determine whether you are presenting a corporate persona which is at odds with how you want and think that you should be treated by your boss, business colleagues, and upper management in this complex social and behavioral environment.

You might be surprised with what you discover in this process, that you are giving little unintended behavioral clues regarding how your boss or manager should interact and treat you at the office.

It is important to be proactive and accountable for your own destiny as much as you can in this world. So learn how to present the best possible brand image for yourself which helps you play the corporate game in a winning manner.

12 CONCLUSION

In this book we discussed a lot of topics in terms that most people will never approach and voice publicly, which is all power for the course in a fake corporate world. I have definitely spoken with a cynically critical voice during this project, and sometimes by means of a little tongue and cheek caricature of the inner workings of Corporate America.

In writing this book, I am able to step back from myself, vis-à-vis the writing method, and realize the kind of voice that I am incorporating into this creative process.

You need to be able to do this in the corporate world, to step back from the specifics of the office drama, and recognize what is really going on, what game is actually being played in these circumstances. You need to properly identify what the core issue is truly all about and have the analytical wherewithal and mental poise to determinedly step back from your current emotionally susceptible state of mind.

As in most cases, you are too close to it all. You are entirely too involved in the trenches of the fight to appropriately realize and fully understand what is genuinely taking place in the problem situation. There is always some kind of strategic game being played in the background of this decidedly competitive and hostile corporate milieu.

If you take a more detached point of view, and look at these office dramas and problem situations from a game playing perspective, you will realize what role the underlying issues are playing in these corporate games masquerading as legitimate conflicts and concerns within the frenetic ecosystem of the corporation.

This bird's eye viewpoint will help you analyze the situation and all its dynamics much better, and ideally facilitate coming up with multiple options regarding how to best handle these complicated and stressful office dramas and problem situations in the corporate world.

This information and insight derived from a meta perspective where one is almost looking down from a distance at the problem situation in a highly analytical and unemotional manner certainly confers a decision-making advantage to the corporate employee. This attitude and approach will unequivocally help the corporate professional determine how best to play this particular game from an overall strategy standpoint going forward in the corporation.

The thoroughgoing analysis is the foremost methodology available to the corporate professional for handling these difficult and complex problem situations that inevitably arise in the corporate world. This methodological process should provide the blueprint for improving your circumstances and hopefully solving the problem situation altogether at the office. The principal goal is always to resolve the conflict in the most logical and practicable manner while situationally playing the corporate game utilizing a theoretically sound and optimal strategic approach.

This is what I refer to as having the ability to step back from the corporate world and have a Game Playing Mindset. It will be helpful to view the corporate world as a strategic game, this way you won't be so emotionally invested in the nitty-gritty machinations of the Corporate

Game.

It is almost a law of nature that emotional participants make particularly poor game players in the corporate arena. Just remember this idea and always keep it in mind when competing and playing the complex game of social and behavioral warfare also known as organizational politics.

It is important to note here that it is really much easier for me to set forth as an idea and write about as a theoretical point in a book, but really hard to do in actual practice. However, acknowledging this fact means that you will not undervalue just how hard this concept and truism is to master and execute successfully in your personal life and in the war games of the corporate battlefield.

But make no mistake, it is essential that you master this self-evident truth regarding not being an emotional game player in the corporate world. Just keep working at it, and yes it requires extremely hard work in terms of mental discipline and training. But it is absolutely essential to make emotional composure a part of your professional approach and mental strategy inside the corporation.

This hard work on the mental approach to the corporate game has its own rewards in the end for the corporate professional. In fact, taking the time and energy in mastering one's emotions will give the individual a competitive advantage in life as a general rule. And likewise, this mental discipline pays enormous dividends for professionals at the office in the tempestuous world of corporate game playing.

Most human beings never even try to master this skill of psychological stability and emotional composure, many people in the corporate environment will try to master this craft, and some professionals will truly succeed to become expert game players in the corporate world.

You can definitely spot the game players at the office who have mastered this skillset, they are smooth as butter with always keeping their emotional states under control no matter how stressful and complicated the problem situation or office drama becomes to resolve in the thick of battle.

Just keep this Game Playing Mindset in the back of your thought processes at all times on the corporate battlefield, and you will be light years ahead of most of your colleagues in the corporate world. As to the inevitable criticism that I am taking an overly harsh and cynical view of Corporate America. This is probably closer to reality on the ground than the noxious marketing gibberish expounded and promoted endlessly via the stereotypical and overtly cliché corporate value slogans.

I will leave it to the reader to interpret when I am being a little facetious in characterizations about the corporate world that I make in this book. However, you might be surprised about the places where I am exaggerating a point for effect, or actually understating the goings on within the mind-numbingly moronic ideological constructs of Corporate America. As this corporate ecosystem of social and behavioral creatures is one strange mercurial world with a veritable life of its own where rules just seem to make themselves up out of nothingness through the invisible hands of dark matter.

But overall the goal of the book is to make you think a little bit about the prism in which you view Corporate America. As you might be missing a lot of what is really happening because you haven't stepped back from the dark abyss of the corporate environment to see how the game of Corporate America is played in all its wondrously lurid complexity.

You will meet some wonderful human beings in the corporate world, and you will learn a great deal about people, processes, technology, systems, and the various management styles. However, you will also encounter plenty of corporate snakes, small-minded individuals, and more incompetence than you could possibly imagine at the best companies in America.

American Corporations have become soulless, empty bastions of treacherous and duplicitous backstabbing activities as a sport. These corporate playgrounds in the sky have devolved where vagabond drifting employees become anesthetized cogs in the corporate wheel which positively operates with a purpose and mind of its own. The consequences of this dystopian reality is one where these zombified automatons replete with their sellout mentality tread water furiously within the poisonously vacuous corporate culture and ultimately become used up and spit out in a cold mechanized manner like yesterday's news.

You better learn to play the corporate game because American Corporations are all about relentless game playing as a hypercompetitive sport which determines winners and losers on the corporate battlefield. You need to understand this corporate law of nature which dictates that one must learn how to play the strategic game just to survive in this merciless, morally bankrupt world of corporate hyenas, snakes and wolves.

The ethically and ideologically corrupt social and behavioral culture of the American Corporation is no place for naïve little corporate lambs who take everything at face value and don't think in a strategic manner at the office. The individuals who fail to learn and play by the rules of the corporate game will get taken advantage of by their peers who never miss the opportunity to slaughter a corporate lamb in the process of doing business in Corporate America.

We discussed some of the games that take place in the corporate world around the present climate throughout this book, and how best to play these games using strategies and game theory methodologies to better navigate this murky, often hidden world of Corporate America. This behind the scenes game playing *Grim Reaper* eventually knocks on the door of every employee during the course of their professional activities in the corporate world. The dark clouds of corporate game playing permeates all aspects of these social and behavioral relationships within the corporation.

This being the case, you need to think things through very carefully in the corporate world. It is essential to properly analyze situations and incorporate decision-making tools like decision trees and game theory calculations to arrive at clearer decisions with a higher expected value. Otherwise, if you continue to make impulsive, emotionally based decisions at the office you will just not survive in this unsparingly mad world of Corporate America, that will absolutely crush your soul if you let it!

The executives who run these corporations primary priority today is how best to maximize their corporate stock options by any means necessary to increase their overall wealth. These corporate plunderers will borrow from the future with ridiculously bad stock buyback programs to help fuel the constant and incessant short-term thinking exemplified by the hamster wheel of quarterly earnings reports.

These quarterly earnings are one giant charade of corporate game playing at its finest. The quarterly earnings reports are artificially inflated via stock buybacks, short-term planning and thinking, and brazen accounting, debt, and tax shenanigans which loot the corporation like pirates on the high seas during the Middle Ages.

American Corporations and the business community used to stand for investment principles whereby stock buybacks were used when the company's stock was undervalued by the market. However, the purpose of stock buybacks in the current environment is to placate shareholders, boost the quarterly earnings numbers, and juice the stock price to enrich the corporate executives no matter how expensive or overvalued the company's stock is in the marketplace.

There used to be a loyalty contract where employees who worked hard and remained dedicated to the company were rewarded with promotions and job security with a legitimate long-term future. However, the era of working at the same company for 25 to 30 years and receiving a gold watch commemorating this two-way implicit loyalty contract are a vanishing breed in American Corporations during this hollowly bleak era of fake corporate values and insufferably vapid pretend culture.

The corporate value system has completely lost its way, gone off the rails, and has become corrupt to the core of American business culture and philosophy. This corporate value system needs to be overhauled before the competitors in China, South Korea, and Germany completely obliterate American companies in the global business fight for market share and overall survival. American Corporations are literally falling apart at the seams, and many have become second-rate players in the global economy.

The noticeable deterioration of American business dominance all stems from a morally bankrupt business philosophy, an overall broken value system, and a decidedly poor company culture. This set of circumstances is responsible for the thoroughly corrupt, highly corrosive, and openly hostile workplace environment where most employees are working against each other as opposed to working together as a cohesive team towards shared common corporate goals.

Most corporate employees are miserable, and corporate workplaces have become toxic game playing machines. It is quite apparent that the carnage which ensues in the workplace environment with the psychological game playing definitely takes its toll on the losers in the chess match of organizational politics.

This toxic work environment certainly leads to more company job hopping in search of better working conditions for American corporate professionals. This isn't a competitive game characterized by a lot of physical aggression and outright violence; however the mental and psychological warfare is off the charts at these corporations.

These corporate workers constantly jump ship similar to rats at ports of call, taking overall legacy knowledge of the company, along with important department and business unit history, as well as critical organizational information, practices, and procedures with them resembling treasure maps of the buried corporate gold.

In fact, entire floors in Corporate America are completely churned over and replaced every five years like clockwork at major corporations in what amounts to a de facto standard American business practice these days.

In light of the fact that there is so much moving around in the corporate world today, most American Corporations are highly inefficient and poorly run enterprises. These corporations are typically filled with inadequately trained and exceedingly incompetent people who have little institutional knowledge regarding critical historical company processes and core business unit practices.

The companies are absolute bastions of large-scale inefficiencies and massive redundancies. This results in substandard resource utilization on the whole, and horrendous management activities and practices only exacerbates the nature of the problem.

The reality of the situation stands that Corporate America has become a business model based upon mercenary labor which is desperately trying to fill the void of a poor business culture, an inadequate corporate structure, and a systemically flawed strategic business approach pertaining to overall organizational management and philosophy.

The colossal failure of American Business Philosophy is demonstrated quite effectively through the mercenary labor practices of the corporate world.

These once great companies in Corporate America have been reduced to hiring tons of contract workers and outside consultants as a core business strategy. In the end, this is an incredibly inefficient way to run a business all things being equal and speaks volumes about the overall health of American Corporations.

These American Corporations may rationalize that they are saving money via this route, but the truth is that they incorporate this mercenary labor strategy out of necessity, and not because this was a well-thought-out business strategy where they examined the total costs associated with the various models, and chose the best method in the ultimate analysis. Having to rely on a mercenary labor model costs more over the long run, loses and wastes legacy knowledge at the company, and is quite disruptive to business operations and overall organizational efficiencies.

In virtue of this mercenary labor strategy for corporations in our current business paradigm, there are no longer any loyalties being bestowed and exchanged as the norm in Corporate America. The employee pensions have been replaced by 401(k) plans, and company sponsored healthcare plans keep requiring more out of pocket contributions from these vagabonding employees every year.

There is no longer pride in the Corporation as a treasured institution of Americana. In practical terms, tradition has gone out the window just like the fake and vacuous company values that everyone summarily pays lip service to as part of the game playing rules, only to be trampled upon whenever most convenient in the course of conducting business-as-usual corporate shenanigans.

American Corporations really have become a reflection of America as a whole, a divisive, hate-ridden enterprise where selfish individualism and incessant infighting has won out over cooperative group behavior towards common goals, genuine values, and shared sacrifice in seeking out and building long-term value for the organization.[35]

The United States of America is a financially broke caricature of its previous glory, has become a shadow of its former self, and the American Corporation embodies this same halfhearted, short-term thinking and rampant incompetency at its finest, blissfully delusional mindset. The unmistakable truth stands that American Corporations in the main are poorly run from an overall organizational, operations, systems, and strategic planning perspective.

These dying enterprises are thoroughly mismanaged at almost every level within the corporate structure. The American Corporations are all in need of serious reform when one looks deeper into the internals of this American business paradigm, both from a financial analysis and overall outlook, and with regard to a broader management, corporate culture, and leadership standpoint.

The American Corporation is broken, and so are most of the people who work in these vast wastelands of behavioral, ethical, moral, and social mediocrity.

There is little hope for humanity within the American Corporation without some serious self-evaluation, thoughtful introspection, and principled soul-searching process which creates a dramatic paradigm shift from the sicknesses of this perniciously poisonous status quo, and ushers in a new era of greater thinking and behaving in the corporate world.

In order to change course and have a rebirth of American Business Philosophy, major changes are required in the corporate world.

35

https://www.psychologicalscience.org/news/releases/individualistic-practices-and-values-increasing-around-the-world.html;
https://www.verywellmind.com/what-are-individualistic-cultures-2795273; https://dictionary.apa.org/individualism;
https://www.alleydog.com/glossary/definition.php?term=Individualism

The goal is to minimize the need for game playing strategies just to survive in this chaotic environment which definitely takes its inevitable toll on corporate professionals through the course of their careers.

But make no mistake, things must change in Corporate America, because right now the once great American Corporation is dead!

These American Corporations have sold out their last remnants of a value system and have become utterly fake, macabre mausoleums to the once vibrant capitalistic icons which embodied American business excellence of the past.

The United States of America and the American Corporation are simultaneously facing their competitive day of reckoning in the twenty-first century, as they both must adapt and evolve quickly to an ever-changing environment, or fall by the wayside and die a miserable death of irrelevancy on the global stage.

ABOUT THE AUTHOR

John Mark Gray has a MA in Philosophy and an MBA in Business. He has worked in academia, Fortune 500 companies, consulting, and financial markets. He has written many articles and white papers on financial markets and economics. He has a background in Logic & Game Theory and enjoys playing Chess and Poker in his spare time.

www.ingramcontent.com/pod-product-compliance
Lightning Source LLC
Chambersburg PA
CBHW030642220526
45463CB00004B/1616